Dr. Donya Ahmadi

Assistant Professor of International Relations, Department of
International Relations and International Organization,
University of Groningen

Published by Plataforma9
December 2023
Niterói, Brazil
www.plataforma9p9.com
ISBN: 978-65-85267-03-8
Edited by Mirna Wabi-Sabi

OVERLOOKED NO MORE

The Iranian women's rights movement and the case for an intersectional feminist agenda

Dr. Donya Ahmadi

A286n

Ahmadi, Donya

Negligenciadas nunca mais: o movimento iraniano pelos direitos das mulheres e o caso para uma agenda feminista interseccional = Overlooked no more: the Iranian women's rights movement and the case for an intersectional feminist agenda / Donya Ahmadi; tradução Mirna Wabi-Sabi. - 1. ed. - Rio de Janeiro: Plataforma9, 2023.
132p.:11x18 cm.

ISBN 978-65-85267-03-8
Título original: Overlooked no more: the Iranian women's rights movement and the case for an intersectional feminist agenda.

1.Feminismo. 2. Irã. 3. Política. Autor. II.Título. III.Assunto. IV. Wabi-Sabi, Mirna.

CDD: 304
CDU: 141.72

Kethlyn Galdino Pereira – Bibliotecária - CRB-8/10560

Índice para catálogo sistemático:

1. Feminismo. 305.4201

2. Feminismo. 141.72

INDEX

The silent warmth within us

will someday, without a doubt

burst out and become the sun.

- Belief, Siavash Kasrai

ABSTRACT

Iranian women have a rich and long-standing legacy of political activism. The origins of the Iranian women's movement can be traced back to the emergence of independent women's groups and periodicals during the constitutional revolution of the early twentieth century. Despite women's active presence and contributions to global political developments of the past century, contemporary historical narratives, by and large, remain characterized by gender-blindness.

This book problematizes the systemic sidelining of women's causes and contributions, not only in the field of historiography, but in Iranian politics at large. It shows that throughout the twentieth century, women's bodies repeatedly emerged as sites of political contestation while their causes were simultaneously instrumentalized and erased from the masculinist political debate. It ultimately posits that the gendering of history constitutes a vital first step towards developing an Iranian intersectional feminist agenda.

INTRODUCTION:
Women in Contemporary Iranian Activism

On International Women's Day on 8 March 1979, only weeks after the victory of the revolution that overthrew the Shah, thousands of Iranian women marched the snowy streets of Tehran. Disillusioned with the new revolutionary council's dubious and discriminatory stances towards women, they took to the streets to demand the preservation of their meagre but hard-earned rights and chanted 'In the dawn of freedom, women have no freedom'. The images of masses of women protesters, many of whom had previously marched the streets in support of the revolution, shocked the world as they rapidly circulated media outlets across the globe.

What had fueled this spontaneous expression of collective anger was a series of direct attacks on women's rights launched by the new regime which included the suspension of an important piece of family legislation that had improved women's divorce and reproductive rights, and the barring of women from becoming judges. The final nail in the coffin was hammered a day before the march, when Ayatollah Khomeini pronounced that women civil servants should wear the hijab in their place of work.

The events of International Women's Day of 1979 marked the beginning of a long and ongoing struggle for gender equality in post-revolutionary Iran. The seeds of this resistance, however, had been planted nearly seven decades before, a fact that is often historically overlooked. The majority of hitherto historical writings on contemporary Iran have, in fact, failed to account for the important role played by women's activism in shaping modern Iranian politics and society.

Writing gender and women back into the history of Iranian mobilization highlights Iranian women's long legacy of political activism. It builds on and contributes to an existing body of work by women historians who have embarked on the essential task of combatting the 'gender-blindness' which characterizes not just contemporary historical narrations of Iranian activism but the field of historiography in general. Gendering historicization cannot be achieved through the mere annexing of women's names, stories, and images to the existing male-centric historical narratives. Rather, it requires the re-introduction of gender as a category of analysis from the onset, in a way that fundamentally transforms historicization itself (Najmabadi, 1996).

By tracing the origins of the Iranian women's movement in the constitutional revolution of the early twentieth century, an overview of women's major political activities throughout various stages of political development in contemporary Iran takes form. Meanwhile, the coercion and cooptation periods of the women's movement under the Pahlavi I and II eras respectively cannot be overlooked. By closely examining the role and position of women in political opposition groups of the revolutionary period and their subsequent activism and repression in the years following the 1979 revolution, a common thread is traced through all major political developments of the past century. The promises and pitfalls of the women's movement carry lessons for the future of feminist activism within and outside Iran.

A HISTORY OF
THE WOMEN'S MOVEMENT IN IRAN

Afsaneh Najmabadi once aptly referred to the general model of historicization in contemporary Iran as one of *"Great Men and Grand Ideas"* (1996: 102). Much has been written about Iran's modernization from above since the early 1900s as well as its grassroots histories of conscientization and political activism. These historical narrations are heterogenous and often-times contested in their claims, reflecting ideologies and standpoints from all over the political spectrum. What unites these diverse historical plots, however, is the systemic and effective downplaying, and at times complete erasure, of the role of women (in particular rural, tribal, and working-class women) and their political claims from the collective national memory, rendering modern Iranian historiography centralist, elitist, and undeniably masculinist.

The Constitutional Movement

The origins of the Iranian women's movement can be traced back to early 20th century. During the Constitutional movement of 1906-1911, the emergence of secret and semi-secret women's councils marked the birth of a new radical women's movement which contributed considerably to the revolutionary cause (see Bayat-Philipp, 2013; Paidar, 1995; Afary, 1989; Sanasarian, 1982; Bamdad, 1977). Janet Afary (1989, 1996) has offered valuable insights on the role played by women of that era in line with Iran's constitutional plight in general, and the fight for women's emancipation in particular. According to her, early Iranian feminists of the constitutional period,

> "often confronted the male leadership of the Constitutional Revolution on social and political issues. Women supported the new parliament but also spoke against the inaction of the delegates. Without any institutional support, they created a network of associations, schools for girls, and hospitals, and they actively contributed to the political debates in the country. On a number of occasions, they challenged the conservative wing of the Ulama (clerics) as well as the delegates to the parliament. The women of Azerbaijan took up

arms and participated in the resistance move-
ment during the 1908-09 civil war of Tabriz.
During the years 1909-11, women affiliated with
the influential social democratic tendency raised
issues that are considered feminist demands to-
day, such as critiques of easy male divorce and
polygyny" (1989: 67).

The early women's movement during the constitutional period, in spite of the general lacking of basic political and social rights accorded to women at the time, was perhaps the most radical women's movement Iran has known to this date. On October 6th, 1906, the first Iranian parliament (Majles) opened, following a series of strikes and sit-ins starting two months prior, which ultimately compelled Muzaffar Al-Din Shah to grant the Iranian nation a right to a parliament as well as a constitution. The latter was ratified by the Qajar monarch on 30 December 1906 (Abrahamian, 1979).

The elitist leadership of the first constitutional period viewed the movement as an *Iranian enlightenment project* (Najmabadi, 1996), or a move towards *democracy along European lines* (Afary, 1989). After the formation of the first Majles, in criticism of foreign influence and financial dependence, women organized extensively around the issue of creating a national bank (Bayat-Philipp, 2013). A formal petition on behalf of female education and civic participation was presented to the

Majles as early as December, 1906. Even though the petition was met with strong opposition at the Majles, by 1913, around 50 girls' schools are reported to have been established in the capital city of Tehran, owing to the organization of Iranian women, particularly through the formerly mentioned women's councils (Ibid).

Since their inception in the first constitutional period, grassroots women's councils had received fierce opposition from the conservative clerics, who deemed the political activities of the women's councils, particularly the issue of women's education, contrary to Islamic beliefs. Some, such as anti-constitutionalist cleric Sheykh Fazlollah Nuri, went so far as to issue religious fatwas against the opening of schools for girls, thereby greenlighting attacks against the young female students and their teachers among religious opponents to girls' schooling (Paidar, 1995; Afary, 1989).

It would, however, be misleading to present the conservative clergy and their fanatical followers as the only opponents of female emancipation. Save for a few male intellectuals and delegates to the Majles, the Constitutional government and its parliament offered meagre to no support to the women's movement, and on many occasions actively opposed their claims. Paidar (1995) contends that the issue of women's societal position remained a highly sensitive topic for conservative anticonstitutionalists and pro-constitutionalists alike, despite their clashing views and opposing stances on other political issues.

With the support of the male delegates sympathetic to the female cause, however, women's demands were occasionality presented to the Majles. The issue of women's councils was originally presented to the first Majles in March 1908, weeks before its closure in the aftermath of a coup d'état staged by Mohammad-Ali Shah with the help of the Russian Cossack brigade. The petition received a degree of support among the more liberal delegates. The debate in the Majles ultimately contended that these women's councils were not to be deemed 'un-Islamic', so long as their nature remained non-political (Afary, 1989).

In the summer of 1909, following a year of activism and resistance, particularly in Tabriz, to which women contributed fiercely, the Majles was re-instated. During the years 1909-1911, what is commonly regarded as the second Constitutional period, the women's movement became even more vocal in addressing gendered injustice. Issues such as divorce and polygyny were problematized in the writings and organizing efforts of individual and collective women alongside the strive for female education.

In August 1911, Vakil-Al-Ru'aya, a liberal delegate from the city of Hamedan who had remained loyal to the women's cause, presented a petition to the second Majles on behalf of women's suffrage (Afary, 1989). This incident is widely recalled in historical narrations of the Constitutional period as a dramatic moment, owing both to the radical nature of the petition posed by Vakil-Al-Ru'aya, as well as the turmoil it appears to have caused in the Majles.

Taking the tribune, Vakil-Al-Ru'aya had declared that since women possessed rights and souls, they should have the right to vote. Facing a bewildered Majles, he then turned to Shaykh Asadullah, a key member of the Ulama, for validation. The conservative cleric, however, *"denied to women either souls or rights and declared that such doctrine would mean the downfall of Islam"* (Afary, 1989: 77). A formal petition was then put forth by the president of the Majles that the entire incident be removed from the house's records. An alternative transcript was instead drafted and presented to the press which recounted the incident as such:

> *"Shaykh Asadullah had not condemned women to a lack of soul; rather, his opinion was based on women's supposed inferior political judgement: 'The reason for excluding women is that God has not given them the capacity needed for taking*

part in politics and electing the representatives of the nation. They are the weaker sex and have not the same power of judgment as men have. However, their rights must not be trampled upon, but must be safeguarded by men as ordained in the Koran by God Almighty'" (1989: 77).

The issue of women's suffrage did not gain spotlight again in the Majles until 1959 (Sanasarian, 1982). In December 1911, the second Constitutional regime came to an end and the Majles was once again forcibly closed following threats of Russian invasion (Afary, 1989).

Notwithstanding the setbacks faced by the women's movement due to the fall of the Constitutional government, women's councils continued to grow in numbers and influence well into the 1930s. In the following decades, women published many periodicals and magazines that specifically discussed women's rights, particularly pertaining to issues of education and veiling. These publications contributed greatly to the construction of the identity of the modern Iranian woman (see also Najmabadi, 1993; Kashani-Sabet, 2005).

Reza Shah Pahlavi and Modernization from Above

In 1914, 1921, and 1923 respectively, the third, fourth and fifth Majles convened. Each, however, closed prematurely due to a chaotic political scene and a disintegrating central government. Following the dissolution of the Qajar dynasty, a strong centralized state was established by Reza Pahlavi. A military officer from the northern region of Mazandaran, Reza Khan initially rose to power as minister of war, following a coup in 1921. In 1923, he was appointed prime minister, and crowned as the Shah of Iran in 1925 (Abrahamian, 2021).

Paidar (1995) posits that the establishment of the Pahlavi dynasty marked a fundamental change in the nature and direction of Iranian nationalism, from a domain of independent political activism to one of state dominance and centralized bureaucracy, with its pro-military leadership and particular vision for building a uniform nation. Reza Shah effectively suppressed all independent political activity, including that of the grassroots women's councils. In June 1931, a law passed forcibly through the Majles by Reza Shah officially banned all political activity deemed 'communist and anti-monar-chical' (Sanasarian, 1982: 67).

The last independent women's organization, Jamiat-e Nesvaan-e Vatankhaah-e Iran (The Patriotic Women's League of Iran), was reportedly banned in 1932. Two years later, a centralized women's organization called Kanoon-e-Banovan (the Society for women) was es-tablished with direct government oversight, with the aims of both depoliticizing the women's movement and advancing areas pertaining to women's emancipation that were in line with Reza Shah's vision for Iranian mo-dernity (Mahdi, 2004). The society later became an important vessel for promoting Reza Shah's controver-sial unveiling decree (Bamdad, 1977).

The unveiling policy of 1936 shocked the conservative fabric of Iranian society and polarized intellectuals and women's activists alike. While official state memoranda reported an overwhelmingly positive public reception of this law, wide-spread opposition to forceful unveiling quickly became apparent. The resistance to the decree notwithstanding, forceful implementation of the veil ban and police surveillance around the issue resulted in the further isolation of many women, particularly among the working classes and the elderly. It is not sur-prising that after the fall of Reza Shah, many such women, who had found themselves at the receiving end of the establishment's coercive measures, went back to using the veil.

Kashani-Sabet has referred to the unveiling decree as a quintessential symbol of Reza Shah's top-down women's renewal program (tajaddod-e-nesvan). The modern Iranian woman, she argues, was a re-incarnation of the archetypal patriotic woman: "*though unveiled, [she] could neither escape the cult of domesticity nor the burdens of patriotic womanhood*" (2005: 45). Much of Reza Shah's advancements in the area of women's emancipation were, in fact, aligned with this renewed vision of a patriotic woman. She was depoliticized, domesticated, and above all, remained loyal to the state-led nationalist cause.

The depoliticization and centralization of women's organizations under Reza Shah's reign thus went hand-in-hand with further domesticizing their activities. While issues such as women's schooling and female hygiene remained central areas of focus, government-sanctioned women's organizations ventured into the new arena of 'charitable work'. Several factors justified the favoring and systemic pursuit of charity in the Pahlavi era: It mobilized (if not exploited) the readily available labor of women with little to no economic costs; effectively limited the scope of their activities in line with what was deemed appropriate by the dominant patriarchal culture; and further reinforced an image of Iran as a modernizing nation (Sanasarian, 1982).

Reza Shah's coercive rule came to a halt in 1941. Following an allied occupation in the aftermath of World War II, Reza Shah abdicated the throne in favor of his son, Mohammad Reza Pahlavi, and was exiled from Iran. In the period immediately following, Iran witnessed an upsurge in the number of political parties and their membership.

New women's organization were founded, often in direct connection to broader political parties. The old Kanoon Banovan, albeit much less visible with Reza Shah's departure, continued to be royal to the Pahlavi establishment, pursuing its domesticizing activities by conducting classes on matters such as literacy, sewing, cooking, etiquette and 'proper' behavior (Ibid.). While the newly established women's organizations enjoyed political independence from the government and assumed more radical stances on women's rights, their close association with broader (masculinist) political parties often resulted in the side-lining of issues pertaining to women's emancipation since broader political goals such as economic restructuring and nationalization of resources automatically took precedence over women's concerns.

In August 1953, a CIA backed coup against the nation-alist prime minister Mohammad Mossadeq marked the beginning of yet another era of political repression and censorship, this time under the rule of Mohammad Reza Shah Pahlavi.

Mohammad Reza Shah and
The White Revolution

Eliz Sansarian (1982) has rightfully dubbed Mohammad Reza Shah's period the *"cooptation and legitimation"* phase of the Iranian women's movement (pg 79). Following in his father's footsteps, Mohammad Reza Shah continued to centralize women's organizations by expanding and supporting those that operated strictly as charitable organizations, and banning and prosecuting the non-charitable organizations that refused to depart from their political activities. Sanasarian (1982) further posits that,

> *"while Reza Shah had coerced activist women into the government, his son encouraged organizational cooptation whereby all women would come under a central institution for women. [...] Coercion involved a use of brute force in the face of opposition; co-optation contained some force but mainly a great deal of political arm twisting"* (81).

Much like his father, Mohammad Reza Shah pursued women's emancipation partially and in line with his modernization plan for the country. The issue of women's suffrage constituted one of the pillars of Mohammad Reza Shah's modernization program, commonly known as The White Revolution, and was ultimately realized on February 27, 1963 following a referendum on the six-point reforms proposed by the Shah. In the same year, six women were elected into the Majles as deputies; two more were appointed by the Shah as senators. In 1965, for the first time in Iranian history, a female minister was appointed. The appointment of women as public officials once again reinforced the image of Pahlavi-era Iran as a country on route to modernization (Ibid.).

While many historical accounts have credited the modernization program of the Pahlavi era exclusively with achieving female enfranchisement, it was, in fact, the decades-long activism of women that had paved the way for many of Mohammad Reza Shah's reforms to align with women's emancipation.

Women's organizations had been campaigning and organizing around the right to vote since the constitutional era. In the decades following Reza Shah's exile, women's suffrage and equal rights proliferated as important focal points among women's organizations, including the Iranian Women's Party (later transformed into the National Council of Women) which lobbied sympathetic deputies to support female suffrage when the issue of electoral reform was raised in the Majles in 1944.

Some political organizations, such as the communist Tudeh party and the Democratic Party of Azarbaijan, further took active stances on the issue of women's civic rights, including that of female enfranchisement. In the 1940s, the Democratic Party of Azarbaijan created an autonomous provincial government in Azerbaijan whereby women were granted the right to participate in elections for the first time in Iranian history.

The Tudeh party, similarly adjusted its constitution to reflect and incorporate the demands of its sister organization, the Democratic Association of Women (Tashkilat Democratic Zanan), including the right to vote. In 1944, the Tudeh faction within the Majles introduced a bill to extend women's right to vote, which was once again dubbed anti-Islamic and not debated (Paidar, 1995).

Other prominent parties, such as Mohammad Mosaddeq's National Front (Jebheye Melli), did not present a united front on the issue of electoral reform, owing to the varied and at times clashing ideologies that existed within the nationalist party. While socialist wings within the National Front such as the Iran Party viewed equality between men and women as fundamental to their political organizing, conservative religious fractions continued to fiercely oppose female suffrage.

The secular nationalist wing and other middle-of-the-way parties of the National Front often did not prioritize women's rights and social reforms over the nationalist cause (Ibid.). Mosaddeq himself admittedly worked towards maintaining the status quo in internal affairs, fearing that socio-economic reforms would cause 'great tension' and undermine 'the struggle on the foreign front' (Siavoshi, 1990: 57).

As Paidar (1995) rightfully posits, women's enthusiasm and eager participation in the struggle for the nationalization of oil,

> *"far exceeded the ability or willingness of the independent nationalist leadership to tackle issues related to women's rights and liberties"* (134).

The nationalist movement thus did not result in any major reforms concerning the position of the Iranian women.

The Great Civilization and Family Reforms

The last decade of Pahlavi rule in Iran witnessed an even stronger emphasis towards state modernization, this time by revoking images of 'The Great Civilization' with reference to the glory days of the ancient Persian Empire. Like its predecessors, the state nationalism of the late Pahlavi era had a strong gendered dimension. Perhaps the most radical achievements on behalf of the women's rights movement in this period concerned family reforms.

In 1967, a bill was presented to the Majles which proposed legal reforms on matters such as divorce, polygyny and child custody. The bill which became widely known as the Family Protection Law was later amended in 1975 to raise the legal age of marriage from fifteen to eighteen for women and further restrict the conditions under which male polygamy was legally allowed. In 1977, abortion up to 12 weeks of pregnancy was declared legal (Paidar, 1995).

While the state prided itself in their newly assumed revolutionary stance towards women's emancipation, the legislations in the area of family reform in the 1960s and 1970s often stemmed from other pressing and contradictory pressures as opposed to a coherent gender policy (Azari, 1983). Paidar (1995) posits that the family reforms implemented in this period were by and large motivated by an increasing urge to curb the rapid growth of population, as well as its economic and political implications.

Their motives notwithstanding, the reformed family laws undoubtedly brought about major positive change in the lives of women who had access to the law. However, they did not transform the dominant patriarchal structure that ruled over Iranian society, nor did they aim to.

The modernization program of Mohammad Reza Shah further impacted Iranian women across various social strata in drastically different ways. While middle-class and affluent women in urban centers such as Tehran benefitted from the new socio-political rights accorded to them, the land reforms and the consequent rapid urbanization exacerbated exploitation and repressive conditions faced by most rural and working-class women.

Reza Shah's efforts towards creating a uniform Iranian identity and centralized bureaucracy had initiated a breakdown of the tribal structure in much of rural Iran. The land reforms implemented by Mohammad Reza Shah in the 1960s as part of his White Revolution program further resulted in the loss of agricultural work in villages. This carried grave consequences for the economic role and social status of rural women.

Rural agricultural work in Iran had traditionally based the family as its basic unit of production, whereby women assumed an active role in the production, control, and distribution of up to 90 percent of all daily household necessities (Paidar, 1995). Modernization and land reform changed the area of female productive activity from the public to the domestic realm. Rural women who had previously assumed productive roles in agricultural fields became confined to the feminized realms of spinning or carpet weaving.

Importantly, rural women's new economic contributions as carpet weavers not only did not result in their emancipation but further subordinated their domestic position, since their labor was mostly unpaid and they owned neither the means of production nor their produce (Afshar, 1985; 1981).

Tabari (1980) similarly contends that the need for female and child labor on peasant family plots increased considerably as a direct result of land reform. The male members of the family often migrated to the urban areas in search of construction or industrial jobs, leaving behind women and younger children to work on the fields.

Partial mechanization of farm labor did not lessen women's burden in the field, since it often did not concern the share of the work which was traditionally the women's domain in the peasant division of labor; namely weeding, cotton-picking, fruit picking, the planting of rice, and harvesting (Tabari, 1980; see also Najmabadi, 1987).

The increasing dependence of most peasant families on child labor further reinforced the patriarchal role of the rural woman as the bearer of children and *"producer of the hands of labor"* (Tabari, 1980: 21). Thus, in the domestic realm, the traditional role of the peasant woman as a mother was prioritized over her productive role, while the economic contribution of her husband strengthened his authoritative role as the patriarchal head of the family.

Similarly, the impact of modernization on the lives of urban women varied significantly depending on their socio-economic class. While much of the existing scholarship on the changing position of urban women in this period has celebrated the positive developments in middle-to-upper-class women's access to education, health care and amenities, the position of urban women from lower strata, including rural women who migrated to towns in search of education or employment, remains largely ignored.

The lower-class working women in urban centers either found employment outside the home as domestic workers, cooks, cleaners, and factory workers, or worked at home as seamstresses, beauticians, and hairdressers. These women had little job security, tended to work long hours under harsh conditions, and were paid less than men. They further received little to no protection from sexual harassment and economic exploitation by employers.

As for urban women of middle-to-upper socio-economic strata, their employment rates fluctuated considerably in the two decades prior to the revolution. Paidar (1995) posits that Iranian middle-class women, despite their outwardly projected image as emancipated working women, were in fact leaving work in the 1970s.

She further identifies a number of social and economic factors which contributed to the decline in women's economic activity in this period including prejudice and opposition by male family members, limited employment opportunities, workplace discrimination such as stereotyping, underpayment, and sexual harassment. Women were thus integrated into the economy in sub-ordinate ways.

The state's inability to fulfill the promise of female emancipation through education and employment opportunities on the one hand, and the conservative patriarchal pressures on women as bearers of the honor of the family and the nation on the other, compelled Iranian women to seek empowerment in various and at times contradicting ways.

Some well-educated women left work in favor of the *"eternal protection and security of the house of a father and later a husband"*, where they claimed their traditional roles as housewives, albeit grossly over-qualified ones (Ibid.: 166). Many found empowerment in joining existing political forces such as the Tudeh party, the Fada'iyan guerillas and other secular opposition groups on the left. These women remained at the forefront of the struggle for gender equality by organizing women at workplaces and urging their respective organizations to allocate political and organizational attention to the struggles of women. Others sought emancipation within the familiar Islamic framework, either by modifying the traditional concepts or retreating to them as a defense mechanism (Tabari, 1980).

Women and Marxist Political Opposition

In the last decade before the revolution, Iran witnessed a stark increase in the number of oppositional political groups working towards the overthrow of the monarchy. While most groups identified with Marxism, their approaches to political action (armed versus non-violent), transnational affiliation and correspondence (especially in relation to the Soviet Union), and religion (Islamic versus secular) varied considerably. All organizations, however, gathered under the umbrella of anti-imperialism and played a significant role in mobilizing different cadres among the Iranian intelligentsia and the working classes that was key to the success of the 1979 revolution.

Among the various grass-roots Marxist groups who participated in the revolutionary cause, three were particularly influential, namely the Tudeh party of Iran (The Masses party of Iran), the Fada'iyan guerillas (Sazman-e Cherik-ha-ye Feda'i-ye Khalq-e Iran), and the Mojahedin Khalgh (Sazman-e Mojahedin-e Khalq-e Iran).

Of the three, the Tudeh party was the longest existing organization with strong transnational ties (with the Soviet Union as well as other grass-roots communist organizations in the Middle-East and Central Asia). Formed by a circle of young Marxist intellectuals in Tehran in the 1940s, the party grew into a momentous national movement within two years of its formation. It has a considerable following among the intelligentsia and working classes, with visible branches in the northern cities, and with clandestine cells in the southern British-occupied regions.

The Tudeh party is further credited for establishing the foundations of trade unionism in Iran. Its Central Council of United Trade Unions is claimed to have had over 355,000 enrolled members by mid-1946 (Abrahamian, 1970). Following the suppression of political organizations after the 1953 Coup, the party was driven mostly underground and partly into exile, whereby it continued its operations and political organizing until the 1979 revolution.

In the 1960s, the Pahlavi regime's extreme use of violence to suppress independent political voices compelled the opposition, particularly its younger members, to question the effectiveness of traditional modes of resistance such as street demonstrations and labor strikes. Unlike the Tudeh party, whose primary approach to political organization remained non-violent, the newly formed organizations became staunch advocates of armed struggle and guerrilla warfare.

The Fada'iyan group officially came into existence in 1971 but it's origins can be traced back to the formation of a guerilla group in 1964 by five Tehran University students, two of whom were former Tudeh members. The group developed an extensive criticism of existing political organizations. They criticized the Tudeh party for prioritizing political struggle and organizational survival over an armed struggle, and underestimating the grievances and concerns of ethnic minorities, particularly in Azerbaijan and Kurdistan (Abrahamian, 1985).

The Mojahedin Khalgh had its origins in the mid-1960s. While the Fada'iyan group evolved predominantly from the Tudeh party and the leftist wing of Mosaddeq's National Front, the Mojahedin Khalgh developed out of the religious wing of the National Front (Ibid.). In developing their ideological standpoints, the group emphasized the revolutionary potential of Shi'i ideology in mobilizing the masses.

Despite their Islamic tendencies, the Mojahedin Khalgh were not fundamentally different from the Fada'iyan in their ideological and practical approaches to revolutionary political action. Both groups were heavily influenced by Marxism, problematized Western imperialism and advocated for a class-less society achieved through a revolution of the masses inspired and facilitated by armed struggle (Abrahamian,1989).

Between the years 1971 and 1975 each group had planned and carried out a series of armed operations. The Fada'iyan had, among others, organized armed rob-beries of five banks, assassinated two police informants, a millionaire industrialist and the chief military prosecu-tor, and bombed the embassies of Britain, Oman, and the United States, as well as the police headquarters of six cities (Abrahamian, 1985).

The Mojahedin Khalgh had bombed Tehran's electrical plant; attempted to hijack an Iranian airplane; carried out arm robberies in six banks; assassinated a US mili-tary adviser and the police chief of Tehran; attempted to assassinate a US general; and bombed a number of symbolic and strategic locations including Reza Shah's mausoleum, and the 'British Overseas Airways' and 'British Petroleum and Shell' offices (Ibid).

By 1976, both groups had suffered such heavy losses that they began to reconsider their revolutionary tac-tics. Following heated internal debates on the issue of armed struggle, the Fada'iyan split into two separate factions. One group continued to carry out armed mis-sions until the 1979 revolution, while the other avoided armed confrontations, increased political activity and established closer ties with the Tudeh party. The latter group came to be known as the Fada'iyan Monshaeb and merged completely with the Tudeh party after the revolution.

The Mojahedin Khalgh, which by then had already split into two separate 'Islamic' and 'Marxist' factions due to ideological differences, also increased their non-violent political activities especially among university students and laborers, publishing journals and strengthening their transnational ties (Ibid.).

Analyzing the role of women in the revolutionary activities of Marxist opposition groups in the years following up to the revolution proves challenging on multiple grounds. Despite the notable role played by these groups in modern Iranian politics, their history remains by and large understudied, and is subject to bias and misrepresentation from all sides of the political spectrum. The existing conflicts among these groups, which grew exponentially in the decade following the revolution, has further contributed to the distortion of important facts and historical accounts.

Raising necessary gendered critique while not falling prey to political propaganda surrounding these groups is not an easy task. Historians of the Iranian women's movement are not an exception to this reality. Parvin

Paidar (1995), for instance, in her significant volume on the role of women in the 20th century political struggles of Iran, perhaps the most exhaustive contribution on the subject to date, downplays the role played by the Tudeh party in the revolutionary period and goes so far as to accuse the group of being "*a traitor among the left*" (169), "*alienated from left solidarity*" (205) and dependent upon Soviet funding and support (249). Such misconstruction, deliberate or not, brings into question the integrity of this otherwise comprehensive contribution to the field of gendered historiography in Iran.

The second challenge in narrating the role and contributions of women affiliated with grass-roots opposition groups concerns the fact that the limited body of work available on the history of these organizations is either completely gender-blind or fails to address gendered aspects in any comprehensive or meaningful way. This is on the one hand due to the dominant masculinist forces in operation within these groups, and on the other due to the side-lining of the category of gender within the field of historiography itself. In fact, in much of the work available on Marxist opposition groups, including accounts of oral and written history provided by the members themselves, the recognition of women's contributions does not go beyond a mere headcount of female members who were arrested or executed in the revolutionary period.

The limitations in historiography notwithstanding, it is evident that women, despite their widespread involvement and contribution at the Rank-And-File level, did not enjoy much autonomy in these opposition groups. Even though all groups advocated the equality of rights for men and women, the promise of gender equality did not materialize beyond the level of lip service and into a feminist problematization of the patriarchy or the material roots of gendered oppression in Iran. In fact, the woman issue was continuously sidelined in favor of the more 'pressing' causes of anti-imperialism and class struggle.

The taken for granted assumption here was that once the issue of capitalist exploitation was solved, women's emancipation would inherently follow suit. Thus, despite their revolutionary Marxism, these groups never ideologically took issue with patriarchal gendered relations and at times dismissed the women's rights question as a western bourgeoisie construct. As a result, women activists often found themselves caught between the conflicting necessities of supporting the father organization and voicing their own gender-specific demands (Afshar, 1985).

Paidar (1995) is right in arguing that female members were often subjected to gendered stereotypes and double standards since they were expected to perform their female duties alongside being freedom fighters. Moreover, the masculinization of female members was deemed the remedy for the objectification and hyper-sexualization of women in the capitalist system:

> *"The Marxist-Leninist woman dressed similarly to her male comrade, wore her hair short, did not use make up and avoided wearing high-heeled shoes. She was encouraged to be tough and to suppress her emotions"* (171).

This masculinization in appearance and behavior could, on the one hand, be considered an unprecedented transgression of traditional binary gendered expressions in Iranian society. On the other hand, it signifies the existence of a politics of respectability within the Marxist opposition not all different from that of the dominant patriarchal culture, since it reflects the essentialist conceptions of woman as hyper-sexual, corrupting, emotional, and irrational, a view propagated by the Pahlavi administration and conservative Islamists alike.

While the Marxist and guerilla movements undoubtedly played a key role in raising critical consciousness and mobilizing against the dictatorship of the Shah, they failed to produce a comprehensive strategy to address the concerns and grievances of Iranian women. This failure manifested more clearly after the 1979 revolution with the refusal of the left to take a firm stance against the new Islamic regime's discriminatory legislation and approach towards women. Overviewing the political developments in the decade following the revolution reveals the grave consequences they carried for the socio-political position of the Iranian woman, as well as the future of political activism under the newly formed Islamic Republic.

The 1979 Revolution and its Aftermath

By the fall of 1978, a decade of political activism against the Pahlavi regime had blossomed into a revolutionary mass uprising. A year before, the Shah, under pressure from the Carter administration as well as international human rights organizations, and in a desperate attempt to regain control over the political order, had introduced a careful program of political liberalization. In the following months, many political prisoners were released and the rules regarding the trial of political dissidents in military courts were amended. The loosening of the grip over political control and the subsequent fall of the Shah's single-party political system had achieved the opposite results the Shah had hoped for.

The liberalization in politics, albeit limited in nature and degree, had activated political opposition against the regime to an unprecedented degree. In the fall of 1978, mass strikes and demonstrations had grown to such an extent that the Shah had to resort to forming a military government to regain control over the political order.

The use of military force and introduction of curfews, however, proved ineffective in containing the country-wide revolutionary momentum, resulting in the Shah's forceful departure from the country.

In February 1979, the military withdrew its support from Bakhtiar, the last prime minister appointed by the shah, and a new provisional government was formed under the supervision of the Council of Islamic Revolution and the leadership of Ayatollah Khomeini (Abrahamian, 1978; 2018).

Women's participation in the revolutionary uprisings of 1979 was historically unprecedented. In the final months leading up to the overthrow of the monarchy, the Anti-Shah movement had succeeded in mobilizing Iranian women from all social classes. In turn, women became the first group whose rights came under direct attack by the newly established Islamic government. The Family Protection Act of 1975 was the first comprehensive legislation of the Pahlavi Era to be abolished as part of the new regime's Islamization policy.

In the following weeks, the new government announced a range of new developments targeting gendered relations and women's civic rights; by the end of March 1979, only weeks after the victory of the revolution, women had been barred from becoming judges, abortion had been declared illegal, sports had become segregated and coeducation had been banned.

In the summer of 1979, a Council of Experts (Majles e Khobregan), comprising mostly of religious figures, was formed to ratify a secretly drafted constitution, a document which provided the legal basis for the establishment of theocratic rule under the direct oversight of Ayatollah Khomeini as the Supreme Guardian (vali e Faghih). The constitution made every democratic right granted individuals conditional on its compatibility with 'Islamic principles', without sufficient clarification of what these principles were.

In most cases, the decision of whether such Islamic principles were preserved was left to the subjective interpretation of a Faqih (religious scholar). The draft further included a number of articles specifically addressing gendered relations and a woman's position in Islamic society. Despite strong opposition by the majority of leftist and secular nationalist forces, as well as ethnic and religious minorities, a final version of the constitution was approved following a referendum in December of 1979 (Azari, 1980).

Much like the constitution of 1906, the constitution of 1979 viewed women predominantly within the context of the family and emphasized the centuries-old patriar-chal role of woman as wife and mother. The only major difference between the two constitutions on women's rights concerned the issue of female suffrage. Khomeini, himself, had strongly opposed women's suffrage when the issue was raised by women under the Pahlavi regime in the 1960s. The new constitution, however, strategically preserved women's right to vote so as to secure Islamist women's support for the new regime.

The new government's unfavorable position towards women did not go unchallenged. Following a speech by Ayatollah Khomeini, in which he declared that women employees of the state should wear the Islamic hijab in their workplace, thousands of women took to the streets on International Women's Day on 8 March 1979, in a collective expression of anger and dismay at what they rightfully deemed an attack on their hard-earned rights.

While Iranian women were already organizing a rally in observance of the International Women's Day in the weeks prior, Khomeini's speech acted as a catalyst for the spontaneous declaration of their grievances. A crowd of nearly 30,000 women were reported to have marched the streets of Tehran on the day (Azari, 1980).

Over the next two days, multiple marches and rallies were organized by women in Tehran and several other cities. These women demonstrators were targeted by mobs of religious zealots who subjected them to a wide range of physical and verbal abuse, including sexual insults, rock throwing, beating, and even stabbing.

By March 11, the rise in casualties and fears of infiltration by counter-revolutionary forces compelled some organizing parties to call the protests to a halt. Nevertheless, a group of some 20,000 women still joined the day's demonstrations. As the march proceeded, protesters were attacked by fanatical mobs armed with weapons, ultimately forcing them to disperse in order to avoid further escalation and clashes with them (Millet, 1982).

The responses of the government to women's mass mobilization were multifold. The national television, which initially had refused to cover the news regarding women's protests, began to show footage of the demonstrations. The coverage, however, was heavily biased in favor of the Islamization policies and discredited the demonstrators as traitors of the revolution by associating them with the Shah and SAVAK (the Shah's intelligence and security organization).

Prime Minister Mehdi Bazargan proclaimed that Ayatollah Khomeini's message had been misinterpreted and reassured women that the government did not have plans to make the hijab compulsory. Abbas Amir Entezam, the government's spokesman and deputy premier, further announced that women civil servants were not required to wear the veil in the workplace but to dress with dignity and modesty, and that the Family Protection Act would remain in force until replaced by new legislation (Sanasarian, 1982; Paidar, 1995).

Despite the initial reconciliatory remarks, the regime continued its attacks on women's rights under the disguise of Islamization. While the women's demonstrations had not attracted the mass support they had hoped for, they had succeeded in exposing the new regime's refusal to accommodate political dissent at a very early stage, a reality which the opposition ignored at first but was later forced to come to terms with once it suffered its devastating consequences.

Women's opposition to regressive policies continued to manifest itself through the emergence of numerous women's groups and organizations. Some organizations were founded independently, and others were formed under the umbrella of broader political groups such as the Tudeh party and the National Front. Many occupation-based women's groups were further formed at workplaces, such as the well-known Association of Women Lawyers which was founded immediately after the revolution in response to reforms in the judiciary, especially in respect to female judges.

The multiplicity of these women's groups and their adoption of localized or profession-based frameworks, however, meant that the already heterogenous post-revolutionary women's movement was becoming more fragmented. It was in this context of fragmentation and 'atomization' that the government saw an opportunity to further its Islamization program and attack on women's rights (Tabari, 1980: 29).

Another important factor which contributed to the further undermining of the women's movement, as rightfully pointed out by Sanasarian (1982), was the presence of deep-rooted cultural and social resistance to women's equality among not just the conservative but also the more moderate wing of the political establishment. The views of 'Progressive' men such as Mehdi Bazargan, Ayatollah Taleghani, and Abolhassan Banisadr on women were, in actuality, not radically different from those held by conservative Islamists. As a result, their token support of the women's movement was superficial at best.

Unfortunately, the Marxist left also fell short in supporting the women's cause, and on a number of occasions even denounced their demonstrations as being part of a counter-revolutionary conspiracy. The dominant masculinist tendencies within the Marxist opposition, once again, resulted in the prioritization of the 'greater' cause of preserving the revolution over women's rights.

From all sides of the political spectrum, women received the message that their concerns were not to be made into a priority but to remain a mere distraction in the great post-revolutionary masculinist struggle over political power.

In the months following the March protests, the regime continued to tighten its hold on the political opposition. In August 1979, the last of the major national newspapers which was not controlled by the establishment was forcefully shut down. The headquarters of the Fada'iyan and Mojahedin Khalgh were further taken over and their publications declared illegal. Gangs of religious zealots continued to regularly harass and attack leftist book stalls, offices and demonstrations (Azari, 1980).

By June 1981, state suppression had successfully eradicated all forms of open political dissent within the country; the opposition had been driven underground or into exile, and thousands of opponents and activists had been imprisoned and many others murdered. The eight-year long war with Iraq helped further consolidate the state by providing it with a highly potent rallying cry.

It also provided an opportunity for the religious militias to transform into a fully-fledged military force named the Army of Revolutionary Guards (Sepah e Pasdaran e Enghelabi), bringing the total number of the Islamic regime's armed forces to more than half a million.

The regime's suppression of political activism continued throughout the years of war. Between 1981 and 1985, more than 8,000 opponents were executed by the revolutionary courts. The victims included members of the Mojahedin, Fada'iyan, Tudeh, National Front, and Kurdish activists. Many, including Tudeh leaders, were forced to appear on national Television to recant their former political views.

The final bloodletting occurred immediately after the end of the war in 1988, when more than 2,800 political prisoners were executed without a trial within a four-week time span and their bodies dumped in mass graves. By the time of Khomeini's death in June 1989, his Islamic republic had been purged of all signs of leftist and secular nationalist opposition (Abrahamian, 2018).

The decade of political suppression, which has come to be known in contemporary Iranian history as the reign of terror, took a severe toll on the women's movement. As mentioned earlier, the majority of women activists had been affiliated with Marxist (and to a lesser degree secular nationalist) groups, and thus bore the same punishment as their male counterparts for being 'criminal offenders'. After the annihilation of Marxist and secular nationalist forces, it was the Islamic opposition's turn.

The Islamic women's movement, which had become increasingly vocal on women's issues and lobbied extensively for the preservation of legal rights granted to women in the immediate years after the revolution, was intimidated into silence. In the late 1980s, a moderate and much less vocal faction of the Islamic women's movement re-emerged. While the early Islamic feminists such as Azam Taleghani and Zahra Rahnavard had adamantly refused to associate themselves with the secular women's movement, they were critical of the forceful imposition of the hijab and advocated their own ideas of Islam's 'true' vision for women in society. The later renditions of the Islamic women's movement, however, proved even more limited in scope and reach.

The government's hypersensitivity to the issue of gender, along with the continued violent suppression of any form of political opposition over the past three decades have undermined the women's movement to the point of near annihilation. Women's activism within Iran has been atomized and individualized to an unprecedented degree. It is, therefore, definitionally impossible to identify a comprehensive women's movement in the post-war decades.

The objectives pursued by women activists inside Iran have further varied considerably depending on the political climate, ranging from lobbying for the improvement of family laws and women's constitutional rights, to campaigning for the release of political prisoners. The temporary rise to power of moderates such as Khatami and Rouhani allowed for limited articulations of women's demands, but always in the face of opposition from the dominant conservative forces who were eager to undo any achievements made on behalf of women as soon as they regained control over the state.

A recent example of this is the passing of a new law under Raisi, the current president of the Islamic Republic, in 2021 which prohibits public health-care providers from offering free contraception and bans voluntary sterilization. This is considered a huge set-back to Iranian women's bodily autonomy and integrity, and their years of activism in the area of reproductive rights, the consequences of which, particularly on those most vulnerable such as young girls and victims of sexual abuse, will only unravel in the years to come.

Despite these limitations, Iranian women continue to resist oppressive gendered structures. Recently, the Iranian women's movement has branched out into new exciting political directions in exile. The emergence of new modes of communication and the rising popularity of social media have helped to mobilize a new generation of Iranian feminists both within and outside the country.

Social media has provided an important platform for the collective articulation of women's concerns and launching consciousness raising and educational campaigns on gendered issues. For the first time, Iranian feminism has adopted an intersectional lens, building alliances with queer and trans activists, and advocating on issues pertaining to racial, ethnic and religious minorities.

The emergence of the Iranian #MeToo movement also provided an unprecedented opportunity for Iranian women of various backgrounds to publicly share accounts of sexual abuse, laying bare the overwhelming extent of the gendered violence experienced by women across social strata. In some cases, the exposure of sexual offenders even resulted in their arrest and prosecution within Iran (Ahmadi, 2023).

The birth of the Woman, Life, Freedom movement, following the brutal killing of Jina (Mahsa) Amini while in the custody of the Iranian morality police in September 2022, has further opened a new and notable chapter in

Iranian feminist activism. Dubbed as Iran's feminist revolution, the ongoing movement adopts the Kurdish feminist slogan of Jin, Jiyan, Azadi to prioritize gendered demands, particularly the right to bodily autonomy for Iranian women and gender non-conforming folk, utilizing innovative modes of everyday resistance (Ibid).

These new waves of feminist activism and solidarity building, although in their early stages of development, are promising new grounds for the furthering of women's political causes and challenging the masculinist forces that have hitherto dominated both the political status quo and its opposition.

CONCLUDING REMARKS

Narrating the political activities of Iranian women throughout the past century shows that women's participation in political affairs in Iran did not begin with their mass presence in the street demonstrations resulting in the overthrow of the Shah in 1979. Rather, it was decades of organizing, mobilizing, and bargaining on behalf of women activists that activated masses of women and paved the way for their visible involvement in the revolutionary events.

Historical accounts often bypass this important legacy of the twentieth century Iranian women's movement, crediting Khomeini's charismatic leadership as the sole contributing factor to the mass mobilization of women, particularly those from working-class and conservative backgrounds. Such reductionist tales recall orientalist essentialism, which portrays Muslim women as passive recipients of politics, who blindly follow the authority of religious men in their pursuit of political power. This book shows that Iranian women have been all but passive victims, and that their political contributions and organizing have been key to any progress made on be-half of socio-political movements in contemporary Iran.

Since the 1980s, significant steps have been taken by women historians towards combatting the patchwork nature of Iranian women's political history. These efforts notwithstanding, dominant historical narratives continue to frame the role of women in the political developments of twentieth century Iran as mere 'participation' at best.

The evolving nationalist and Islamist discourses around which major political developments of the century were organized by and large regarded women as objects of protection rather than political subjects. Afsaneh Najmabadi's important work on the story of the daughters of Quchan has shed light on such historical blind spots by tracing the gendered origins of Iranian nationalism (1996; 1998). Najmabadi posits that throughout the Constitutional movement, the notion of 'country' (vatan) emerged as a feminized entity whose autonomy depended on the protection of patriarchal and patriotic men. The 'nation' (mellat) was, in turn, masculinized as the agentic subject tasked with protecting both the sovereignty of the country and the purity of her women.

Nationalist discourses of the Constitutional era thus instrumentalized the female body (and its corresponding Vatan), so as to create widespread sympathy for the causes of nationalism and constitutionalism. This instrumentalization did not result in the improvement of women's oppressive conditions or the centralization of their cause in the broader Constitutionalist movement. In fact, women's stories and political contributions were effectively wiped from the historicization and collective memory of the constitutional era once they had served their purpose in line with mobilizing mass nationalist sentiments.

Throughout the twentieth century, women's bodies continued to emerge as contested ideological and political battlegrounds. This is especially evident with respect to the issue of the hijab. Reza Shah's forceful imposition of the unveiling decree polarized Iranian society and women's rights activists alike. It added fuel to the conservative clergy's opposition to the modernization of women's social position who framed women's emancipation as a cry for secularization and de-Islamization.

Reza Shah, in turn, cracked down on the independent women's movement and depoliticized its demands. He later created a centralized government-sanctioned women's association that would control and channel women's political activities in line with his top-down modernization plan, while continuing the coercive suppression of politically affiliated women's organizations and individual activists.

Mohammad Reza Shah followed in his father's foot-steps by further centralizing women's organizations and repressing independent political activity. Unlike Reza Shah who responded to political dissent by resorting primarily to violent coercion, Mohammad Reza Shah used both the carrot and the stick in his cooptation of the women's movement. Those women activists who sided with the monarch's modernizing plans were absorbed into the state apparatus whereby they continued to lobby for legal improvements of women's conditions. Two notable achievements on behalf of the centralized women's movement during the Pahlavi II era could be regarded as female enfranchisement and the Family Protection Act of 1975.

As the last Shah of the Imperial State, Mohammad Reza adopted a divide and conquer strategy in responding to the women's movement. As a result, women activists were pitted against one another and further divided along ideological and class lines. This eradicated any and all possibilities for coalition-building among women and the centralization of women's concerns in the broader political movements of the Pahlavi II era.

The same pattern of fragmentation and polarization can be observed among the female members of political opposition groups in the pre-revolutionary period. While the ideological differences between the royalist women and women activists on the opposition side, particularly on the left, were often irreconcilable, leftist women shared enough ideological common ground to form a united front in organizing around the female cause. This was, unfortunately, not achieved due to the existence of petty rivalries among Marxist opposition groups on which these women activists depended.

On the intra group level, Marxist opposition groups refused to prioritize women's issues over the more immediate revolutionary causes of anti-Imperialism and fighting class inequality, and their responses to women's concerns remained piecemeal and tokenistic. This genderblind approach of the Marxist opposition continued throughout the early years of the post-revolution era and was finally challenged once the Islamic regime fully enforced its discriminatory laws against women.

Similarly, during the 1979 revolution, women's bodies once again re-surfaced as politicized grounds on which the Islamic revolutionary forces would 'revert' the Shah's modernization efforts. The post-revolutionary regime's Islamization program targeted women's bodies and social relations specifically. Opposing the sexism of the new regime disguised as Islamization was, in turn, framed as 'anti-revolutionary' and pro-west. Religious figures who had previously praised women's heroic participation in the revolutionary events and boasted women's high status in an Islamic society, emerged as staunch opponents of women's emancipation once in power.

Much like during Reza Shah's reign, the issue of veiling became a focal point in the new regime's efforts towards consolidating its power. Both regimes targeted women's rights to bodily autonomy and resorted to forceful and repressive measures to curtail resistance and ensure mass compliance. Thus, a recurring theme that can be observed at various stages of contemporary Iranian history is the weaponization of women's causes and concerns by political stakeholders, irrespective of their religious and political standings, towards their own political gains, and the subsequent sidelining and erasure of women's causes once they no longer served the broader masculinist political agendas. It is thereby evident that gender has always been simultaneously politicized and erased from the political debate, a pattern which continues to this very date.

Re-writing the contemporary histories of mobilization from below, by re-centering the stories and narratives of those whose voices and struggles have been rendered irrelevant, remains a hefty but vital political task. Drawing from the power and wisdom of shared experience, Iranian feminists are able to re-evaluate the political ways of our foremothers and re-articulate our political demands in line with a radical liberating praxis. There are, moreover, important lessons to be drawn from women's social justice struggles across the globe.

Black feminists' invaluable teachings on intersectionality and the interconnected ways in which various axes of power and privilege shape women's identities and lived experiences remain notable sources of inspiration. History shows us time and again that social justice movements that fail to problematize their inner hierarchies of power can themselves become sites where coercive power structures get reproduced. The adoption of narrow single-axis approaches to political organizing, as was the case with Marxist opposition groups in pre and post-revolutionary Iran, further results in the peripheralization of the voices of women, ethnic minorities and queer folk, and undermines the sustainability of the movement and the radical nature of its demands. Only through the pursuit of a truly intersectional feminist praxis and solidarity building across various classes, genders, sexualities, and ethnicities can the Iranian women's movement unleash its true transformative potential.

REFERENCES

Abrahamian, E. (2021). *Iran between two revolutions*. Princeton University Press.

Abrahamian, E. (2018). *A history of modern Iran*. Cambridge University Press.

Abrahamian, E. (1989). *The Iranian Mojahedin*. Yale University Press.

Abrahamian, E. (1985). The guerrilla movement in Iran, 1963–77. In *Iran* (pp. 149-174). Palgrave Macmillan, London.

Abrahamian, E. (1979). The causes of the constitutional revolution in Iran. *International Journal of Middle East Studies*, 10(3), 381-414.

Abrahamian, E. (1978). Iran: the Political Challenge. In *Middle East Report*, no. 69, July-August.

Abrahamian, E. (1970). Communism and communalism in Iran: The Tudah and the Firqah-i Dimukrat. *International Journal of Middle East Studies*, 1(4), 291-316.

Afary, J. (1996). *The Iranian Constitutional Revolution, 1906-1911*. New York.

Afary, J. (1989). On the origins of Feminism in early 20th-century Iran. *Journal of Women's History*, 1(2), 65-87.

Afshar, H. (1985). *Women, Work, and Ideology in the Third World*. London: Tavistock.

Afshar, H. (1981). The Position of Women in an Iranian Village. In *Feminist Review*, no. 9.

Ahmadi, D. (2023). Standing on top of society's sexist load: Gatekeeping activism and feminist respectability politics in the case of the Iranian MeToo Movement. In *Women's Studies International Forum*, 99, 102765.

Azari, F. (1983). *Women of Iran: The Conflict with Fundamentalist Islam*. London: Ittaca Press.

Bamdad, B. A. M. (1977). *From Darkness Into Light: Women's Emancipation in Iran*. Edited and translated by F. R. C. Bagley. New York: Exposition Press.

Bayat-Philipp, M. (2013). 15 Women and Revolution in Iran, 1905-1911. In *Women in the Muslim world* (pp. 295-308). Harvard University Press.

Kashani-Sabet, F. (2005). Patriotic womanhood: The culture of feminism in modern Iran, 1900–1941. *British Journal of Middle Eastern Studies, 32*(1), 29-46.

Mahdi, A. A. (2004). The Iranian women's movement: A century long struggle. *The Muslim World, 94*(4), 427-448.

Millett, K. (1982). *Going to Iran*. Coward, McCann & Geoghegan.

Najmabadi, A. (1998). *The story of the daughters of Quchan: Gender and national memory in Iranian history*. Syracuse University Press.

Najmabadi, A. (1996). "Is our name remembered?": Writing the history of Iranian constitutionalism as if women and gender mattered. *Iranian Studies, 29*(1-2), 85-109.

Najmabadi, A. (1993). Zanha-yi Millat: women or wives of the nation? *Iranian Studies, 26*(1-2), 51-71.

Najmabadi, A. (1987). *Land reform and social change in Iran* (pp. 50-168). Salt Lake City: University of Utah Press.

Paidar, P. (1995). *Women and the Political Process in Twentieth-Century Iran*. Cambridge Middle East studies, Vol. 1.

Sanasarian, E. (1982). *The Women's Rights Movement in Iran Mutiny, Appeasement, and Repression from 1900 to Khomeini*. New York: Praeger.

Siavoshi, S. (1990). *Liberal Nationalism in Iran: The Failure of a Movement*. Boulder: Westview Press.

Tabari, A. (1980). The enigma of veiled Iranian women. *Feminist Review*, 5(1), 19-31.

Dra. Donya Ahmadi

Professora de Relações Internacionais, Departamento de
Relações Internacionais e Organização Internacional,
Universidade de Groningen

Publicado pela Plataforma9
Dezembro 2023
Niterói, Brasil
www.plataforma9p9.com
ISBN: 978-65-85267-03-8
Edição e tradução: Mirna Wabi-Sabi
Revisão de texto: Nox Morningstar

NEGLIGENCIADAS NUNCA MAIS

O movimento iraniano pelos direitos das mulheres e o caso para uma agenda feminista interseccional

Dra. Donya Ahmadi

A286n

Ahmadi, Donya

Negligenciadas nunca mais: o movimento iraniano pelos direitos das mulheres e o caso para uma agenda feminista interseccional = Overlooked no more: the Iranian women's rights movement and the case for an intersectional feminist agenda / Donya Ahmadi; tradução Mirna Wabi-Sabi. - 1. ed. - Rio de Janeiro: Plataforma9, 2023.
132p.:11x18 cm.

ISBN 978-65-85267-03-8
Título original: Overlooked no more: the Iranian women's rights movement and the case for an intersectional feminist agenda.

1.Feminismo. 2. Irã. 3. Política. Autor. II.Título. III.Assunto. IV. Wabi-Sabi, Mirna.

CDD: 304
CDU: 141.72

Kethlyn Galdino Pereira – Bibliotecária - CRB-8/10560

Índice para catálogo sistemático:

1.   Feminismo. 305.4201

2.   Feminismo. 141.72

ÍNDEX

O calor silencioso dentro de nós

um dia, sem dúvida

irrompeu e tornou-se o sol.

- Belief (Crença), Siavash Kasrai

RESUMO

As mulheres iranianas têm um legado de ativismo político rico e duradouro. As origens do movimento das mulheres iranianas remontam ao surgimento de grupos e periódicos independentes de mulheres durante a revolução constitucional do início do século XX. Apesar da presença ativa e das contribuições das mulheres para os desenvolvimentos políticos globais do século passado, as narrativas históricas contemporâneas, em geral, permanecem caracterizadas pela cegueira de gênero.

Esse livro problematiza a marginalização sistêmica das causas e contribuições das mulheres, não apenas no campo da historiografia, mas na política iraniana em geral. Mostro que, ao longo do século XX, os corpos das mulheres repetidamente emergiram como locais de contestação política, enquanto suas causas foram simultaneamente instrumentalizadas e apagadas do debate político masculinista. Em última análise, postulo que o gênero da história constitui um primeiro passo vital para o desenvolvimento de uma agenda feminista interseccional iraniana.

INTRODUÇÃO:
Mulheres no Ativismo Iraniano Contemporâneo

No Dia Internacional da Mulher, em 8 de março de 1979, apenas algumas semanas após a vitória da revolução que derrubou o xá (ou Shah), milhares de mulheres iranianas marcharam pelas ruas nevadas de Teerã. Desiludidas com as posturas dúbias e discriminatórias do novo conselho revolucionário em relação às mulheres, elas foram às ruas para exigir a preservação de seus escassos, mas duramente conquistados direitos e cantaram, "No alvorecer da liberdade, as mulheres não têm liberdade". As imagens da multidão de mulheres manifestantes, muitas das quais já haviam marchado nas ruas em apoio à revolução, chocaram o mundo à medida que circulavam rapidamente nos meios de comunicação global.

O que alimentou essa expressão espontânea de raiva coletiva foi uma série de ataques calculados lançados pelo novo regime aos direitos das mulheres, que incluíam a suspensão de uma peça importante da legislação

familiar que havia melhorado o divórcio e os direitos reprodutivos das mulheres, e a proibição de mulheres se tornarem juízas. O último prego no caixão foi martelado um dia antes da marcha, quando o aiatolá (ou Ayatollah) Khomeini pronunciou que as funcionárias públicas deveriam usar o hijab no local de trabalho.

Os eventos do Dia Internacional da Mulher de 1979 marcaram o início de uma longa e contínua luta pela igualdade de gênero no Irã pós-revolucionário. As sementes dessa resistência, no entanto, foram plantadas quase sete décadas antes, um fato que muitas vezes é historicamente esquecido. A maioria dos escritos históricos sobre o Irã contemporâneo, de fato, falhou em explicar o papel notável desempenhado pelo ativismo das mulheres na formação da política e da sociedade iraniana moderna.

Escrever sobre gênero e mulheres na história da mobilização iraniana destaca o longo legado de ativismo político das mulheres iranianas. O texto se baseia e contribui para um corpo de trabalho existente de mulheres historiadoras que embarcaram na tarefa importante de combater a "cegueira de gênero" que caracteriza não apenas as narrativas históricas contemporâneas do ativismo iraniano, mas o campo da historiografia em geral. A historicização de gênero não pode ser alcançada por meio da mera anexação de nomes, histórias e imagens

de mulheres às narrativas históricas existentes, centradas no homem. Em vez disso, ela requer a reintrodução do gênero como uma categoria de análise desde o início, de uma forma que transforma fundamentalmente a própria historicização (Najmabadi, 1996).

Ao traçar as origens do movimento das mulheres iranianas na revolução constitucional do início do século XX, uma visão geral toma forma das principais atividades políticas das mulheres em vários estágios de desenvolvimento político no Irã contemporâneo. Enquanto isso, os períodos de coerção e cooptação do movimento de mulheres sob as eras Pahlavi I e II, respectivamente, não podem ser negligenciados. Ao examinar de perto o papel e a posição das mulheres nos grupos de oposição política do período revolucionário e seu subsequente ativismo e repressão nos anos seguintes à revolução de 1979, um fio comum é traçado em todos os principais desenvolvimentos políticos do século passado. As promessas e armadilhas do movimento de mulheres trazem lições para o futuro do ativismo feminista dentro e fora do Irã.

UMA HISTÓRIA DO MOVIMENTO DE MULHERES NO IRÃ

Afsaneh Najmabadi uma vez se referiu apropriadamente ao modelo geral de historicização no Irã contemporâneo como um dos "Grandes Homens e Grandes Ideias" (1996: 102). Muito foi escrito sobre a modernização do Irã desde o início de 1900, bem como suas histórias de base de conscientização e ativismo político. Essas narrativas históricas são heterogêneas e muitas vezes contestadas em suas reivindicações, refletindo ideologias e pontos de vista de todo o espectro político. O que une essas diversas tramas históricas, no entanto, é a subestimação sistêmica e efetiva, e, às vezes, o apagamento completo, do papel das mulheres (em particular, mulheres rurais, tribais e da classe trabalhadora) e suas reivindicações políticas da memória nacional coletiva, tornando a historiografia iraniana moderna centralista, elitista e, inegavelmente, masculinista.

O Movimento Constitucional

As origens do movimento das mulheres iranianas remontam ao início do século XX. Durante o movimento constitucional de 1906–1911, o surgimento de conselhos de mulheres secretos e semi-secretos marcou o nascimento de um novo movimento radical de mulheres que contribuiu consideravelmente para a causa revolucionária (ver Bayat-Philipp, 2013; Paidar, 1995; Afary, 1989; Sana-sarian, 1982; Bamdad, 1977). Janet Afary (1989, 1996) ofereceu informações valiosas sobre o papel desempenhado pelas mulheres daquela época em consonância com a situação constitucional do Irã em geral e a luta pela emancipação das mulheres em particular. Segundo ela, as primeiras feministas iranianas do período constitucional,

> "muitas vezes, confrontavam a liderança masculina da Revolução Constitucional em questões sociais e políticas. As mulheres apoiaram o novo parlamento, mas também se manifestaram contra a inércia dos delegados. Sem qualquer apoio institucional, criaram uma rede de associações, escolas para meninas e hospitais, e contribuíram ativamente para os debates políticos do país. Em

várias ocasiões, eles desafiaram a ala conserva-dora dos Ulama (clérigos), bem como os delega-dos do parlamento. As mulheres do Azerbaijão pegaram em armas e participaram do movi-mento de resistência durante a guerra civil de Tabriz de 1908–09. Durante os anos de 1909–11, as mulheres afiliadas à influente tendência so-cial-democrata levantaram questões considera-das demandas feministas hoje, como críticas ao divórcio masculino fácil e à poliginia" (1989: 67).

O movimento das primeiras mulheres durante o perí-odo constitucional, apesar da falta geral de direitos po-líticos e sociais básicos concedidos às mulheres na época, foi talvez o movimento de mulheres mais radical que o Irã conheceu até hoje. Em 6 de outubro de 1906, o primeiro parlamento iraniano (Majles) foi inaugurado, após uma série de greves e protestos iniciados dois me-ses antes, o que acabou obrigando Muzaffar Al-Din Shah a conceder à nação iraniana o direito a um parla-mento, bem como uma constituição. Este último foi ra-tificado pelo monarca Qajar em 30 de dezembro de 1906 (Abrahamian, 1979).

A liderança elitista do primeiro período constitucional via o movimento como um projeto iluminista iraniano (Najmabadi, 1996), ou um movimento em direção à de-mocracia nos moldes europeus (Afary, 1989).

Após a formação dos primeiros Majles, em crítica à influência estrangeira e dependência financeira, as mulheres se organizaram amplamente em torno da questão da criação de um banco nacional (Bayat-Philipp, 2013). Uma petição formal em nome da educação feminina e participação cívica foi apresentada ao Majles já em dezembro de 1906. Embora a petição tenha encontrado forte oposição no Majles, em 1913, cerca de 50 escolas femininas foram relatadas como estabelecidas na capital Teerã devido à organização de mulheres iranianas, particularmente através dos conselhos de mulheres anteriormente mencionados (Ibid.).

Desde a sua criação no primeiro período constitucional, os conselhos populares de mulheres receberam forte oposição dos clérigos conservadores, que consideravam as atividades políticas dos conselhos de mulheres, particularmente a questão da educação das mulheres, contrárias às crenças islâmicas. Alguns, como o clérigo anti-constitucionalista Sheykh Fazlollah Nuri, chegaram ao ponto de emitir fátuas (*fatwas*) religiosas contra a abertura de escolas para meninas, dando assim sinal verde aos ataques contra as jovens alunas e seus professores entre os opositores religiosos à escolaridade das meninas (Paidar, 1995; Afary, 1989).

Seria, entretanto, enganoso apresentar o clero conservador e seus seguidores fanáticos como os únicos oponentes à emancipação feminina. Com exceção de alguns intelectuais do sexo masculino e delegados dos Majles, o governo constitucional e seu parlamento ofereceram pouco ou nenhum apoio ao movimento das mulheres e, em muitas ocasiões, se opuseram ativamente às suas reivindicações. Paidar (1995) afirma que a questão da posição social das mulheres permaneceu um tópico altamente sensível para conservadores anti-constitucionalistas e pró-constitucionalistas, apesar de suas visões conflitantes e posições opostas em outras questões políticas.

Com o apoio dos delegados masculinos simpatizantes da causa feminina, no entanto, as demandas das mulheres eram ocasionalmente apresentadas aos Majles. A questão dos conselhos de mulheres foi originalmente apresentada ao primeiro Majles em março de 1908, semanas antes de seu fechamento após um golpe de estado encenado por Mohammad-Ali Shah com a ajuda da brigada cossaca russa. A petição recebeu certo apoio entre os delegados mais liberais. O debate no Majles, em última análise, sustentou que esses conselhos de mulheres não deveriam ser considerados "anti-islâmicos", desde que sua natureza permanecesse apolítica (Afary, 1989).

No verão de 1909, após um ano de ativismo e resistência, principalmente em Tabriz, para o qual as mulheres contribuíram ferozmente, o Majles foi reinstalado. Durante os anos de 1909–1911, o que é comumente considerado o segundo período constitucional, o movimento das mulheres tornou-se ainda mais vocal ao abordar a injustiça de gênero. Questões como o divórcio e a poliginia foram problematizadas nas escritas e nos esforços de organização de mulheres individuais e coletivas ao lado da luta pela educação feminina.

Em agosto de 1911, Vakil-Al-Ru'aya, um delegado liberal da cidade de Hamedan que permaneceu leal à causa das mulheres, apresentou uma petição ao segundo Majles em nome do sufrágio feminino (Afary, 1989). Esse incidente é amplamente lembrado em narrativas históricas do período Constitucional como um momento dramático, tanto pela natureza radical da petição apresentada por Vakil-Al-Ru'aya, quanto pela turbulência que parece ter causado nos Majles.

Tomando a tribuna, Vakil-Al-Ru'aya declarou que, como as mulheres possuem direitos e almas, elas deveriam ter o direito de votar. Diante de um Majles perplexo, ele então se voltou para Shaykh Asadullah, um membro-chave do Ulama, para validação. O clérigo conservador, no entanto, *"negou às mulheres almas ou direitos e declarou que tal doutrina significaria a queda do*

Islã" (Afary, 1989: 77). Uma petição formal foi então apresentada pelo presidente dos Majles para que todo o incidente fosse removido dos registros da casa. Em vez disso, uma transcrição alternativa foi redigida e apresentada à imprensa, que relatou o incidente como tal:

> "Shaykh Asadullah não condenou as mulheres à falta de alma; ao contrário, sua opinião baseava-se no suposto julgamento político inferior das mulheres: "A razão para excluir as mulheres é que Deus não lhes deu a capacidade necessária para participar da política e eleger os representantes da nação. Elas são o sexo frágil e não têm o mesmo poder de julgamento que os homens. No entanto, seus direitos não devem ser pisoteados, mas devem ser salvaguardados pelos homens conforme ordenado no Alcorão por Deus Todo-Poderoso" (1989: 77).

A questão do sufrágio feminino não voltou a ganhar destaque nos Majles até 1959 (Sanasarian, 1982). Em dezembro de 1911, o segundo regime constitucional chegou ao fim e os Majles foram novamente fechados à força após ameaças de invasão russa (Afary, 1989).

Apesar dos reveses enfrentados pelo movimento de mulheres devido à queda do governo constitucional, os conselhos de mulheres continuaram a crescer em número e influência até a década de 1930. Nas décadas

seguintes, as mulheres publicaram muitos periódicos e revistas que discutiam especificamente os direitos das mulheres, particularmente no que diz respeito a questões de educação e uso do véu. Essas publicações contribuíram significantemente para a construção da identidade da mulher iraniana moderna (ver também Najmabadi, 1993; Kashani-Sabet, 2005).

Reza Shah Pahlavi e a Modernização Autoritária

Em 1914, 1921 e 1923, respectivamente, o terceiro, quarto e quinto Majles se reuniram. Cada um, no entanto, fechou prematuramente devido a um cenário político caótico e um governo central em desintegração. Após a dissolução da dinastia Qajar, um forte estado centralizado foi estabelecido por Reza Pahlavi. Um oficial militar da região norte de Mazandaran, Reza Khan inicialmente subiu ao poder como ministro de Guerra, após um golpe em 1921. Em 1923, foi nomeado primeiro-ministro e coroado Xá do Irã em 1925 (Abrahamian, 2021).

Paidar (1995) postula que o estabelecimento da dinastia Pahlavi marcou uma mudança fundamental na natureza e direção do nacionalismo iraniano, de um domínio de ativismo político independente para um domínio de Estado e burocracia centralizada, com sua liderança pró-militar e visão particular para a construção de uma nação uniforme. Reza Shah efetivamente suprimiu toda

atividade política independente, incluindo a dos conselhos populares de mulheres. Em junho de 1931, uma lei aprovada à força pelos Majles por Reza Shah proibiu oficialmente toda atividade política considerada "comunista e antimonárquica" (Sanasarian, 1982: 67).

A última organização feminina independente, Jamiat-e Nesvaan-e Vatankhaah-e Iran (A Liga Patriótica das Mulheres do Irã), foi banida em 1932. Dois anos depois, uma organização feminina centralizada chamada Kanoon-e-Banovan (a Sociedade para mulheres) foi estabelecida com a supervisão direta do governo, com o objetivo de despolitizar o movimento de mulheres e avançar em áreas pertencentes à emancipação das mulheres que estavam de acordo com a visão de Reza Shah para a modernidade iraniana (Mahdi, 2004). A sociedade mais tarde se tornou um veículo importante para promover o decreto controverso de inauguração de Reza Shah (Bamdad, 1977).

A política de tirada do véu de 1936 chocou o tecido conservador da sociedade iraniana e polarizou intelectuais e ativistas de mulheres. Enquanto os memorandos oficiais do estado relatavam uma recepção pública esmagadoramente positiva dessa lei, a oposição generalizada à tirada forçada do véu rapidamente se tornou aparente.

Apesar da resistência ao decreto, a implementação vigorosa da proibição do uso do véu e a vigilância policial sobre o assunto resultaram no isolamento de muitas mulheres, principalmente entre as classes trabalhadoras e idosas. Não é de surpreender que, após a queda de Reza Shah, muitas dessas mulheres, que se viram na linha de frente das medidas coercitivas do estabelecimento estatal, tenham voltado a usar o véu.

Kashani-Sabet referiu-se ao decreto de tirada do véu como um símbolo quintessencial do programa de renovação de mulheres de cima para baixo, ou autoritário, de Reza Shah (tajaddod-e-nesvan). A mulher iraniana moderna, ela argumenta, era uma reencarnação do arquétipo da mulher patriótica: "*embora sem véu, [ela] não podia escapar do culto da domesticidade nem dos fardos da feminilidade patriótica*" (2005: 45). Muitos dos avanços de Reza Shah na área da emancipação feminina foram, de fato, alinhados com essa visão renovada de uma mulher patriótica. Ela foi despolitizada, domesticada e, acima de tudo, permaneceu leal à causa nacionalista liderada pelo Estado.

A despolitização e a centralização das organizações de mulheres sob o reinado de Reza Shah andaram de mãos dadas com a domesticação de suas atividades. Enquanto questões como a escolaridade das mulheres e a higiene feminina permaneceram como áreas centrais

de foco, as organizações de mulheres sancionadas pelo governo se aventuraram na nova arena do "trabalho de caridade". Vários fatores justificaram o favorecimento e a busca sistêmica da caridade na era Pahlavi: mobilizou (se não explorou) o trabalho prontamente disponível de mulheres com pouco ou nenhum custo econômico; limitaram efetivamente o escopo de suas atividades de acordo com o considerado apropriado pela cultura patriarcal dominante; e reforçou ainda mais a imagem do Irã como uma nação em modernização (Sanasarian, 1982).

O governo coercitivo de Reza Shah foi interrompido em 1941. Após uma ocupação aliada depois da Segunda Guerra Mundial, Reza Shah abdicou do trono em favor de seu filho, Mohammad Reza Pahlavi, tendo sido, então, exilado do Irã. No período imediatamente seguinte, o Irã testemunhou um aumento no número de partidos políticos e seus membros.

Novas organizações de mulheres foram fundadas, muitas vezes em conexão direta com partidos políticos mais amplos. O velho Kanoon Banovan, embora muito menos visível com a partida de Reza Shah, continuou a ser Realeza para o estabelecimento Pahlavi, perseguindo suas atividades domesticadoras ao conduzir aulas sobre assuntos como alfabetização, costura, culinária, etiqueta e comportamento 'adequado' (Ibid.).

Enquanto as recém-estabelecidas organizações de mulheres desfrutavam de independência política do governo e assumiam posições mais radicais sobre os direitos das mulheres, sua estreita associação com partidos políticos mais amplos (masculinistas) muitas vezes resultava na marginalização de questões relativas à emancipação das mulheres, uma vez que objetivos políticos mais amplos como a reestruturação econômica e a nacionalização de recursos automaticamente prevaleceram em detrimento das preocupações das mulheres.

Em agosto de 1953, um golpe apoiado pela CIA contra o primeiro-ministro nacionalista Mohammad Mossadeq marcou o início de mais uma era de repressão política e censura, dessa vez sob o governo de Mohammad Reza Shah Pahlavi.

Mohammad Reza Shah e
a Revolução Branca

Eliz Sansarian (1982) apelidou corretamente o período de Mohammad Reza Shah de fase de "cooptação e legitimação" do movimento das mulheres iranianas (pág.79). Seguindo os passos de seu pai, Mohammad Reza Shah continuou a centralizar as organizações de mulheres, expandindo e apoiando aquelas que operavam estritamente como organizações de caridade e banindo e processando as organizações não beneficentes que se recusavam a se afastar de suas atividades políticas. Sanasarian (1982) postula ainda que,

> "enquanto Reza Shah havia coagido mulheres ativistas a entrar no governo, seu filho encorajava a cooptação organizacional pela qual todas as mulheres seriam submetidas a uma instituição central para mulheres. [...] A coerção envolvia o uso de força bruta em face da oposição; a cooptação continha alguma força, mas principalmente uma grande dose de torção de braço político" (81).

Assim como seu pai, Mohammad Reza Shah buscou a emancipação das mulheres parcialmente e de acordo com seu plano de modernização do país. A questão do sufrágio feminino constituiu um dos pilares do programa de modernização de Mohammad Reza Shah, comumente conhecido como A Revolução Branca, e foi finalmente realizado em 27 de fevereiro de 1963 após um referendo sobre os seis pontos de reformas propostas pelo Xá. No mesmo ano, seis mulheres foram eleitas para o Majles como deputadas; mais duas foram nomeadas senadoras pelo xá. Em 1965, pela primeira vez na história do Irã, uma ministra foi nomeada. A nomeação de mulheres como funcionárias públicas mais uma vez reforçou a imagem do Irã da era Pahlavi como um país a caminho da modernização (Ibid.).

Embora muitos relatos históricos tenham creditado o programa de modernização da era Pahlavi exclusivamente com a conquista do direito de voto feminino, foi, de fato, o ativismo de décadas de mulheres que abriu o caminho para muitas das reformas de Mohammad Reza Shah se alinharem com a emancipação das mulheres.

As organizações de mulheres vinham fazendo campanha e se organizando em torno do direito de voto desde a era constitucional. Nas décadas que se seguiram ao exílio de Reza Shah, o sufrágio feminino e a igualdade

de direitos proliferaram como pontos focais importantes entre as organizações femininas, incluindo o Partido das Mulheres Iranianas (mais tarde transformado no Conselho Nacional das Mulheres), que pressionou deputados simpatizantes para apoiar o sufrágio das mulheres quando a questão da reforma eleitoral foi levantada no Majles em 1944.

Algumas organizações políticas, como o partido comunista Tudeh e o Partido Democrático do Azerbaijão, também assumiram posições ativas na questão dos direitos cívicos das mulheres, incluindo o da emancipação feminina. Na década de 1940, o Partido Democrático do Azerbaijão criou um governo provincial autônomo no Azerbaijão, pelo qual as mulheres receberam o direito de participar das eleições pela primeira vez na história iraniana.

O partido Tudeh também ajustou sua constituição para refletir e incorporar as demandas de sua organização irmã, a Associação Democrática de Mulheres (Tashkilat Democrática Zanan), incluindo o direito de voto. Em 1944, a facção Tudeh dentro do Majles apresentou um projeto de lei para estender o direito de voto das mulheres, que foi mais uma vez apelidado de anti-islâmico e não debatido (Paidar, 1995).

Outros partidos proeminentes, como a Frente Nacional de Mohammad Mosaddeq (Jebheye Melli), não apresentaram uma frente unida na questão da reforma eleitoral, devido às ideologias variadas e às vezes conflitantes que existiam dentro do partido nacionalista. Enquanto alas socialistas dentro da Frente Nacional, como o Partido do Irã, viam a igualdade entre homens e mulheres como fundamental para sua organização política, frações religiosas conservadoras continuaram a se opor ferozmente ao sufrágio feminino.

A ala nacionalista secular e outros partidos intermediários da Frente Nacional muitas vezes não priorizavam os direitos das mulheres e as reformas sociais sobre a causa nacionalista (Ibid.). O próprio Mosaddeq reconhecidamente trabalhou para manter o status quo nos assuntos internos, temendo que as reformas socioeconômicas pudessem causar "grande tensão" e minar "a luta na frente externa" (Siavoshi, 1990: 57).

Como Paidar (1995) corretamente coloca, o entusiasmo e a participação das mulheres na luta pela nacionalização do petróleo,

> *"excedeu em muito a capacidade ou a vontade da liderança nacionalista independente de abordar questões relacionadas aos direitos e liberdades das mulheres"* (134).

O movimento nacionalista, portanto, não resultou em grandes reformas relativas à posição das mulheres iranianas.

A Grande Civilização e as Reformas Familiares

A última década do governo Pahlavi no Irã testemunhou uma ênfase ainda mais forte na modernização do estado, dessa vez revogando as imagens da "Grande Civilização" com referência aos dias de glória do antigo Império Persa. Como seus predecessores, o nacionalismo estatal do final da era Pahlavi tinha uma forte dimensão de gênero. Talvez as conquistas mais radicais do movimento pelos direitos das mulheres nesse período tenham a ver com as reformas familiares.

Em 1967, foi apresentado um projeto de lei aos Majles que propunha reformas legais em questões como divórcio, poliginia e guarda dos filhos. O projeto de lei que se tornou amplamente conhecido como Lei de Proteção à Família foi posteriormente alterado em 1975 para aumentar a idade legal do casamento de quinze para dezoito anos para as mulheres e restringir ainda mais as condições sob as quais a poligamia masculina era legalmente permitida. Em 1977, o aborto até 12 semanas de gravidez foi declarado legal (Paidar, 1995).

Enquanto o estado se orgulhava de sua postura revolucionária recém-assumida em relação à emancipação das mulheres, as legislações na área da reforma familiar nas décadas de 1960 e 1970 muitas vezes resultaram de outras pressões prementes e contraditórias em oposição a uma política de gênero coerente (Azari, 1983). Paidar (1995) postula que as reformas familiares implementadas neste período foram em grande parte motivadas por um desejo crescente de conter o rápido crescimento da população, bem como suas implicações econômicas e políticas.

Apesar de seus motivos, as leis de família reformadas sem dúvida trouxeram grandes mudanças positivas na vida das mulheres que tiveram acesso à lei. No entanto, elas não transformaram a estrutura patriarcal dominante que governava a sociedade iraniana, nem visaram.

O programa de modernização de Mohammad Reza Shah impactou ainda mais as mulheres iranianas em vários estratos sociais de maneiras drasticamente diferentes. Enquanto as mulheres ricas e de classe média em centros urbanos como Teerã se beneficiavam dos novos direitos sociopolíticos concedidos a elas, as reformas agrárias e a consequente rápida urbanização exacerbaram a exploração e as condições repressivas enfrentadas pela maioria das mulheres rurais e da classe trabalhadora feminina.

Os esforços de Reza Shah para criar uma identidade iraniana uniforme e uma burocracia centralizada iniciaram um colapso da estrutura tribal em grande parte do Irã rural. As reformas agrárias implementadas por Mohammad Reza Shah na década de 1960 como parte de seu programa da Revolução Branca resultaram ainda mais na perda de trabalho agrícola nas aldeias. Isso trouxe graves consequências para o papel econômico e o status social das mulheres rurais.

O trabalho agrícola rural no Irã tradicionalmente fundava a família como sua unidade básica de produção, em que as mulheres assumiam um papel ativo na produção, controle e distribuição de até 90% de todas as necessidades domésticas diárias (Paidar, 1995). A modernização e a reforma agrária mudaram a esfera da atividade produtiva feminina do âmbito público para o âmbito doméstico. As mulheres rurais que haviam anteriormente assumido funções produtivas nos campos agrícolas ficaram confinadas aos reinos feminizados da fiação ou da tecelagem de tapetes.

É importante ressaltar que as novas contribuições econômicas das mulheres rurais como tecelãs de tapetes não apenas falharam em resultar em sua emancipação, mas também subordinaram sua posição doméstica, uma vez que seu trabalho não era pago e elas não possuíam

nem os meios de produção, nem seus produtos (Afshar, 1985; 1981).

Tabari (1980) também afirma que a necessidade de trabalho feminino e infantil em lotes de famílias camponesas aumentou consideravelmente como resultado direto da reforma agrária. Os membros masculinos da família muitas vezes migravam para as áreas urbanas em busca de empregos em construção ou na indústria, deixando para trás mulheres e crianças menores para trabalharem nos campos.

A mecanização parcial do trabalho agrícola não diminuiu o fardo das mulheres no campo, uma vez que muitas vezes não dizia respeito à parte do trabalho que era tradicionalmente domínio das mulheres na divisão camponesa do trabalho; ou seja, capina, colheita de algodão, colheita de frutas, plantio de arroz e ceifa (Tabari, 1980; ver também Najmabadi, 1987).

A crescente dependência da maioria das famílias camponesas do trabalho infantil reforçou ainda mais o papel patriarcal da mulher rural como portadora de filhos e "*produtora das mãos do trabalho*" (Tabari, 1980: 21). Assim, no âmbito doméstico, o papel tradicional da camponesa como mãe foi priorizado sobre seu papel produtivo, enquanto a contribuição econômica do marido fortaleceu seu papel autoritário como chefe patriarcal da família.

Da mesma forma, o impacto da modernização na vida das mulheres urbanas variou significativamente dependendo de sua classe socioeconômica. Embora muitos dos estudos existentes sobre a mudança de posição das mulheres urbanas nesse período tenham celebrado os desenvolvimentos positivos no acesso das mulheres de classe média a alta à educação, cuidados de saúde e amenidades, a posição das mulheres urbanas de estratos mais baixos, incluindo mulheres rurais que migraram para as cidades em busca de educação ou emprego, permanece amplamente ignorado.

As trabalhadoras de classe baixa nos centros urbanos encontravam emprego fora de casa como empregadas domésticas, cozinheiras, faxineiras e operárias de fábricas, ou trabalhavam em casa como costureiras, esteticistas e cabeleireiras. Essas mulheres tinham pouca segurança no emprego, tendiam a trabalhar longas horas em condições difíceis e recebiam menos do que os homens. Além disso, receberam pouca ou nenhuma proteção contra assédio sexual e exploração econômica por parte dos empregadores.

Quanto às mulheres urbanas de estratos socioeconômicos médio-alto, suas taxas de emprego flutuaram consideravelmente nas duas décadas anteriores à revolução. Paidar (1995) postula que as mulheres iranianas de classe média, apesar de sua imagem externamente

projetada como mulheres trabalhadoras emancipadas, estavam de fato deixando o trabalho na década de 1970.

Ela ainda identifica uma série de fatores sociais e econômicos que contribuíram para o declínio da atividade econômica das mulheres nesse período, incluindo preconceito e oposição por membros masculinos da família, oportunidades limitadas de emprego, discriminação no local de trabalho, como estereótipos, pagamento insuficiente e assédio sexual. As mulheres foram assim integradas na economia de forma subordinada.

A incapacidade do Estado de cumprir a promessa de emancipação feminina por meio de educação e oportunidades de emprego, por um lado, e as pressões patriarcais conservadoras sobre as mulheres como portadoras da honra da família e da nação, por outro, obrigaram as mulheres iranianas a buscar o empoderamento de formas variadas e, às vezes, contraditórias.

Algumas mulheres instruídas deixaram o trabalho em favor da "*eterna proteção e segurança da casa de um pai e depois marido*", onde reivindicavam seus papéis tradicionais de donas de casa, ainda que de modo geral sobrequalificadas (Ibid.: 166). Muitos encontraram empoderamento unindo-se a forças políticas existentes, como o partido Tudeh, os guerrilheiros Fada'iyan e outros grupos seculares de oposição à esquerda.

Essas mulheres permaneceram na vanguarda da luta pela igualdade de gênero, organizando as mulheres nos locais de trabalho e incitando suas respectivas organizações a alocar atenção política e organizacional às lutas das mulheres. Outras buscaram a emancipação dentro da estrutura islâmica familiar, seja modificando os conceitos tradicionais ou retornando a eles como um mecanismo de defesa (Tabari, 1980).

As Mulheres e a Oposição Política Marxista

Na última década antes da revolução, o Irã testemunhou um grande aumento no número de grupos políticos de oposição trabalhando para derrubar a monarquia. Embora a maioria dos grupos se identificasse com o marxismo, suas abordagens à ação política (armada versus não-violenta), afiliação e correspondência transnacional (especialmente em relação à União Soviética) e religião (islâmica versus secular) variavam consideravelmente. Todas as organizações, no entanto, se reuniram sob a égide do anti-imperialismo e desempenharam um papel significativo na mobilização de diferentes quadros entre a intelectualidade iraniana e as classes trabalhadoras que foram a chave para o sucesso da revolução de 1979.

Entre os vários grupos marxistas de base que participaram da causa revolucionária, três foram particularmente influentes, a saber, o partido Tudeh do Irã (Partido das Massas do Irã), os guerrilheiros Fada'iyan (Sazman-e Cherik-ha-ye Feda'i-ye Khalq-e Irã) e o Mojahedin

Khalgh (Sazman-e Mojahedin-e Khalq-e Irã). Dos três, o partido Tudeh era a organização existente há mais tempo com fortes laços transnacionais (com a União Soviética, bem como outras organizações comunistas de base no Oriente Médio e na Ásia Central). Formado por um círculo de jovens intelectuais marxistas em Teerã na década de 1940, o partido se transformou em um importante movimento nacional dois anos após sua formação. Ele tem um número considerável de seguidores entre as classes intelectuais e trabalhadoras, com ramificações visíveis nas cidades do norte e com células clandestinas nas regiões do sul ocupadas pelos britânicos.

O partido Tudeh é ainda creditado por estabelecer as bases do sindicalismo no Irã. Seu Conselho Central de Sindicatos Unidos teria mais de 355.000 membros inscritos em meados de 1946 (Abrahamian, 1970). Após a supressão de organizações políticas resultante do golpe de 1953, o partido foi levado, em sua maioria, à clandestinidade e parcialmente ao exílio, pelos quais continuou suas operações e organização política até a revolução de 1979.

Na década de 1960, o uso extremo da violência pelo regime de Pahlavi para suprimir vozes políticas independentes obrigou a oposição, particularmente seus membros mais jovens, a questionar a eficácia dos modos

tradicionais de resistência, como manifestações de rua e greves trabalhistas. Ao contrário do partido Tudeh, cuja abordagem primária à organização política permaneceu não-violenta, as organizações recém-formadas tornaram-se defensores ferrenhos da luta armada e da guerrilha.

O grupo Fada'iyan surgiu oficialmente em 1971, mas suas origens remontam à formação de um grupo guerrilheiro em 1964 por cinco estudantes da Universidade de Teerã, dois dos quais eram ex-membros do Tudeh. O grupo desenvolveu uma extensa crítica às organizações políticas existentes. Eles criticaram o partido Tudeh por priorizar a luta política e a sobrevivência organizacional sobre uma luta armada e subestimar as queixas e preocupações das minorias étnicas, particularmente no Azerbaijão e no Curdistão (Abrahamian, 1985).

O Mojahedin Khalgh teve suas origens em meados da década de 1960. Enquanto o grupo Fada'iyan evoluiu predominantemente do partido Tudeh e da ala esquerdista da Frente Nacional de Mosaddeq, o Mojahedin Khalgh desenvolveu-se da ala religiosa da Frente Nacional (Ibid.). Ao desenvolver seus pontos de vista ideológicos, o grupo enfatizou o potencial revolucionário da ideologia xiita na mobilização das massas.

Apesar de suas tendências islâmicas, os Mojahedin Khalgh não eram fundamentalmente diferentes dos Fada'iyan em suas abordagens ideológicas e práticas para a ação política revolucionária. Ambos os grupos foram fortemente influenciados pelo marxismo, problematizaram o imperialismo ocidental e defenderam uma sociedade sem classes, alcançada por meio de uma revolução das massas inspirada e facilitada pela luta armada (Abrahamian, 1989).

Entre os anos de 1971 e 1975, cada grupo planejou e realizou uma série de operações armadas. Os Fada'iyan organizaram, entre outros, assaltos à mão armada de cinco bancos, assassinaram dois informantes da polícia, um industrialista milionário e o principal promotor militar, e bombardearam as embaixadas da Grã-Bretanha, Omã e dos Estados Unidos, bem como as sedes policiais de seis cidades (Abrahamian, 1985).

O Mojahedin Khalgh havia bombardeado a usina elétrica de Teerã; tentou sequestrar um avião iraniano; realizou assaltos à mão armada em seis bancos; assassinou um conselheiro militar dos EUA e o chefe da polícia de Teerã; tentou assassinar um general dos EUA; e bombardearam vários locais simbólicos e estratégicos, incluindo o mausoléu de Reza Shah e os escritórios da 'British Overseas Airways' e da 'British Petroleum and Shell' (Ibid).

Em 1976, ambos os grupos sofreram perdas tão pesadas que começaram a reconsiderar suas táticas revolucionárias. Após debates internos acalorados sobre a questão da luta armada, o Fada'iyan se dividiu em duas facções separadas. Um grupo continuou a realizar missões armadas até a revolução de 1979, enquanto o outro evitou confrontos armados, aumentou a atividade política e estreitou laços com o partido Tudeh. Este último grupo ficou conhecido como Fada'iyan Monshaeb e fundiu-se completamente com o partido Tudeh após a revolução.

O Mojahedin Khalgh, que já havia se dividido em duas facções separadas, 'islâmicas' e 'marxistas', devido a diferenças ideológicas, também aumentou suas atividades políticas não violentas, especialmente entre estudantes universitários e trabalhadores, publicando jornais e fortalecendo seus laços transnacionais (ibid.).

Analisar o papel das mulheres nas atividades revolucionárias dos grupos marxistas de oposição nos anos que se seguiram à revolução é um desafio por vários motivos. Apesar do papel importante desempenhado por esses grupos na política iraniana moderna, sua história permanece, em geral, pouco estudada e está sujeita a preconceitos e deturpações de todos os lados do espectro político. Os conflitos existentes entre esses gru-

pos, que cresceram exponencialmente na década seguinte à revolução, contribuíram ainda mais para a distorção de fatos e relatos históricos relevantes.

Levantar críticas de gênero necessárias sem cair na propaganda política em torno desses grupos não é uma tarefa fácil. Historiadoras do movimento de mulheres iranianas não são uma exceção a essa realidade. Parvin Paidar (1995), por exemplo, em seu trabalho robusto sobre o papel das mulheres nas lutas políticas do século XX no Irã, talvez a contribuição mais completa sobre o assunto até hoje, minimiza o papel desempenhado pelo partido Tudeh no período revolucionário e chega a acusar o grupo de ser *"um traidor da esquerda"* (169), *"alienado da solidariedade de esquerda"* (205) e dependente do financiamento e apoio soviético (249). Essa má interpretação, deliberada ou não, questiona a integridade dessa contribuição abrangente para o campo da historiografia de gênero no Irã.

O segundo desafio em narrar o papel e as contribuições das mulheres afiliadas a grupos de oposição de base diz respeito ao fato de que o corpo limitado de trabalho disponível sobre a história dessas organizações é completamente cego ao gênero ou falha em abordar aspectos de gênero de qualquer forma abrangente, ou significativa. Isso se deve, por um lado, às forças masculinistas dominantes em operação dentro desses grupos e, por

outro, à marginalização da categoria de gênero dentro do próprio campo da historiografia. De fato, em grande parte do trabalho disponível sobre grupos de oposição marxista, incluindo relatos de história oral e escrita fornecidos pelos próprios membros, o reconhecimento das contribuições das mulheres não vai além de uma mera contagem de membros do sexo feminino presos ou executados no período revolucionário.

Apesar das limitações da historiografia, é evidente que as mulheres, apesar de seu amplo envolvimento e contribuição no nível de base, não se aproveitaram de muita autonomia nesses grupos de oposição. Mesmo que todos os grupos defendessem a igualdade de direitos para homens e mulheres, a promessa de igualdade de gênero não se materializou além do nível da boca para fora e em uma problematização feminista do patriarcado ou das raízes materiais da opressão de gênero no Irã. De fato, a questão da mulher foi continuamente deixada de lado em favor das causas mais "prementes" do anti-imperialismo e da luta de classes.

A suposição dada aqui era que, uma vez que a questão da exploração capitalista fosse resolvida, a emancipação das mulheres seguiria inerentemente o exemplo. Assim, apesar de seu marxismo revolucionário, esses grupos nunca questionaram ideologicamente as relações patriarcais de gênero e, às vezes, descartaram a questão dos

direitos das mulheres como uma construção da burguesia ocidental. Como resultado, as mulheres ativistas muitas vezes se viram presas entre as necessidades conflitantes de apoiar a organização paterna e expressar suas próprias demandas específicas de gênero (Afshar, 1985).

Paidar (1995) está certa ao argumentar que os membros do sexo feminino foram frequentemente submetidos a estereótipos de gênero e padrões duplos, uma vez que se esperava que desempenhassem seus deveres femininos ao lado de serem combatentes da liberdade. Além disso, a masculinização dos membros femininos foi considerada o remédio para a objetificação e hiper-sexualização das mulheres no sistema capitalista:

> *"A mulher marxista-leninista vestia-se à semelhança do seu camarada, usava o cabelo curto, não usava maquilhagem e evitava usar sapatos de salto alto. Ela foi encorajada a ser dura e a suprimir suas emoções"* (171).

Essa masculinização na aparência e no comportamento pode, por um lado, ser considerada uma transgressão sem precedentes das tradicionais expressões binárias de gênero na sociedade iraniana. Por outro lado, significa a existência de uma política de respeitabilidade dentro da oposição marxista não muito diferente daquela da cul-

tura patriarcal dominante, uma vez que reflete as concepções essencialistas da mulher como hipersexual, corruptora, emocional, e irracional, uma visão propagada pelo governo Pahlavi e pelos islâmicos conservadores.

Embora os movimentos marxistas e guerrilheiros tenham indubitavelmente desempenhado um papel fundamental na conscientização crítica e na mobilização contra a ditadura do xá, eles falharam em produzir uma estratégia abrangente para abordar as preocupações e queixas das mulheres iranianas. Esse fracasso se manifestou mais claramente após a revolução de 1979, com a recusa da esquerda em assumir uma posição firme contra a legislação discriminatória do novo regime islâmico e sua abordagem em relação às mulheres. Uma visão geral dos desenvolvimentos políticos na década seguinte à revolução revela as graves consequências que eles trouxeram para a posição sociopolítica da mulher iraniana, bem como o futuro do ativismo político sob a recém-formada República Islâmica.

A Revolução de 1979 e Suas Consequências

No outono de 1978, uma década de ativismo político contra o regime de Pahlavi floresceu em um levante revolucionário em massa. Um ano antes, o Xá, sob pressão do governo Carter, bem como de organizações internacionais de direitos humanos, e em uma tentativa desesperada de recuperar o controle sobre a ordem política, havia introduzido um programa cuidadoso de liberalização política. Nos meses seguintes, muitos presos políticos foram libertos e as regras relativas ao julgamento de dissidentes políticos em tribunais militares foram alteradas. O afrouxamento do controle político e a subsequente queda do sistema político de partido único do xá alcançaram os resultados opostos que o xá esperava.

A liberalização na política, embora limitada em natureza e grau, havia ativado a oposição política contra o regime em um grau sem precedentes. No outono de 1978, as greves e manifestações em massa cresceram a tal ponto que o Xá teve que recorrer à formação de um governo

militar para recuperar o controle sobre a ordem política. O uso da força militar e a introdução de toques de recolher, no entanto, mostraram-se ineficazes para conter o ímpeto revolucionário em todo o país, resultando na saída forçada do Xá do país.

Em fevereiro de 1979, os militares retiraram seu apoio de Bakhtiar, o último primeiro-ministro nomeado pelo xá, e um novo governo provisório foi formado sob a supervisão do Conselho da Revolução Islâmica e a liderança do aiatolá (ou Ayatollah) Khomeini (Abrahamian, 1978; 2018).

A participação das mulheres nas revoltas revolucionárias de 1979 foi, historicamente, sem precedentes. Nos últimos meses que antecederam a derrubada da monarquia, o movimento Anti-Shah conseguiu mobilizar mulheres iranianas de todas as classes sociais. Por sua vez, as mulheres se tornaram o primeiro grupo cujos direitos foram atacados diretamente pelo recém-estabelecido governo islâmico. A Lei de Proteção à Família de 1975 foi a primeira legislação abrangente da Era Pahlavi a ser abolida como parte da política de islamização do novo regime.

Nas semanas seguintes, o novo governo anunciou uma série de novos desenvolvimentos visando as relações de gênero e os direitos cívicos das mulheres; no final de

março de 1979, apenas algumas semanas após a vitória da revolução, as mulheres foram proibidas de se tornarem juízas, o aborto foi declarado ilegal, os esportes foram segregados e a educação mista foi proibida.

No verão de 1979, um Conselho de Especialistas (Majles e Khobregan), composto principalmente por figuras religiosas, foi formado para ratificar uma constituição secretamente elaborada, um documento que fornecia a base legal para o estabelecimento do governo teocrático sob a supervisão direta do Ayatollah Khomeini como o Guardião Supremo (vali e Faghih). A constituição condicionou todos os direitos democráticos concedidos aos indivíduos à sua compatibilidade com os "princípios islâmicos", sem esclarecimento suficiente sobre o que eram esses princípios.

Na maioria dos casos, a decisão de se tais princípios islâmicos foram preservados foi deixada para a interpretação subjetiva de um Faqih (estudioso religioso). O rascunho incluía ainda uma série de artigos abordando especificamente as relações de gênero e a posição da mulher na sociedade islâmica. Apesar da forte oposição da maioria das forças nacionalistas seculares e de esquerda, bem como das minorias étnicas e religiosas, uma versão final da constituição foi aprovada após um referendo em dezembro de 1979 (Azari, 1980).

Muito parecido com a constituição de 1906, a constituição de 1979 via as mulheres predominantemente no contexto da família e enfatizava o papel patriarcal secular da mulher como esposa e mãe. A única grande diferença entre as duas constituições sobre os direitos das mulheres dizia respeito à questão do sufrágio feminino. O próprio Khomeini se opôs fortemente ao sufrágio feminino quando a questão foi levantada por mulheres sob o regime de Pahlavi na década de 1960. A nova constituição, no entanto, preservou estrategicamente o direito de voto das mulheres, de modo a garantir o apoio das mulheres islâmicas ao novo regime.

A posição desfavorável do novo governo em relação às mulheres não deixou de ser contestada. Após um discurso do Ayatollah Khomeini, no qual ele declarou que as funcionárias do Estado deveriam usar o hijab islâmico em seus locais de trabalho, milhares de mulheres saíram às ruas no Dia Internacional da Mulher em 8 de março de 1979, em uma expressão coletiva de raiva e consternação com o que eles consideraram um ataque a seus direitos arduamente conquistados.

Enquanto as mulheres iranianas já organizavam uma manifestação em homenagem ao Dia Internacional da Mulher nas semanas anteriores, o discurso de Khomeini atuou como um catalisador para a declaração espontânea de suas queixas. Foi relatado que uma multidão de

quase 30.000 mulheres marchou pelas ruas de Teerã no dia (Azari, 1980).

Nos dois dias seguintes, várias marchas e comícios foram organizados por mulheres em Teerã e em várias outras cidades. Essas mulheres manifestantes foram alvo de multidões de fanáticos religiosos que as submeteram a uma ampla gama de abusos físicos e verbais, incluindo insultos sexuais, arremesso de pedras, espancamento e até facadas.

Em 11 de março, o aumento das baixas e o medo de infiltração de forças contra-revolucionárias obrigaram alguns partidos organizadores a interromper os protestos. No entanto, um grupo de cerca de 20.000 mulheres ainda se juntou às manifestações do dia. À medida que a marcha avançava, os manifestantes foram atacados por multidões fanáticas armadas com armas, forçando-os a se dispersar para evitar uma nova escalada e confrontos com eles (Millet, 1982).

As respostas do governo à mobilização em massa das mulheres foram múltiplas. A televisão nacional, que inicialmente se recusou a cobrir as notícias sobre os protestos das mulheres, começou a mostrar imagens das manifestações. A cobertura, no entanto, foi fortemente tendenciosa em favor das políticas de islamização e de-

sacreditou os manifestantes como traidores da revolução ao associá-los ao Xá e à SAVAK (a organização de inteligência e segurança do Xá).

O primeiro-ministro Mehdi Bazargan proclamou que a mensagem de Ayatollah Khomeini foi mal interpretada e garantiu às mulheres que o governo não tinha planos de tornar o hijab obrigatório. Abbas Amir Entezam, porta-voz do governo e vice-primeiro-ministro, anunciou ainda que as funcionárias públicas não eram obrigadas a usar o véu no local de trabalho, mas a se vestir com dignidade e modéstia, e que a Lei de Proteção à Família permaneceria em vigor até ser substituída por uma nova legislação. (Sanasarian, 1982; Paidar, 1995).

Apesar das observações iniciais de reconciliação, o regime continuou seus ataques aos direitos das mulheres sob o disfarce da islamização. Embora as manifestações das mulheres não tenham atraído o apoio de massa que esperavam, elas conseguiram expor a recusa do novo regime em acomodar a dissidência política em um estágio muito inicial, uma realidade que a oposição ignorou a princípio, mas depois foi forçada a lidar com, uma vez que sofreu suas consequências devastadoras.

A oposição das mulheres às políticas regressivas continuou a se manifestar através do surgimento de organizações e grupos numerosos de mulheres. Algumas organizações foram fundadas independentemente e

outras foram formadas sob a égide de grupos políticos mais amplos, como o partido Tudeh e a Frente Nacional. Muitos grupos de mulheres com base na ocupação foram formados nos locais de trabalho, como a conhecida Associação de Mulheres Advogadas, fundada imediatamente após a revolução em resposta a reformas no judiciário, especialmente no que diz respeito às juízas.

A multiplicidade desses grupos de mulheres e sua adoção de estruturas localizadas ou baseadas em profissões, no entanto, significou que o já heterogêneo movimento pós-revolucionário de mulheres estava se tornando mais fragmentado. Foi neste contexto de fragmentação e 'atomização' que o governo viu uma oportunidade para aprofundar o seu programa de islamização e atacar os direitos das mulheres (Tabari, 1980: 29).

Outro fator importante que contribuiu para enfraquecer ainda mais o movimento das mulheres, como corretamente apontado por Sanasarian (1982), foi a presença de uma resistência social e cultural profundamente enraizada à igualdade das mulheres, não apenas da ala conservadora, mas também da mais moderada do estabelecimento político. As opiniões de homens 'progressistas' como Mehdi Bazargan, Ayatollah Taleghani e Abolhassan Banisadr sobre as mulheres não eram, na verdade, radicalmente diferentes daquelas mantidas por islamitas conservadores. Como resultado,

seu apoio simbólico ao movimento das mulheres foi, na melhor das hipóteses, superficial.

Infelizmente, a esquerda marxista também falhou em apoiar a causa das mulheres e, em várias ocasiões, até denunciou suas manifestações como parte de uma conspiração contrarrevolucionária. As tendências masculinistas dominantes dentro da oposição marxista, mais uma vez, resultaram na priorização da causa 'maior' de preservar a revolução acima os direitos das mulheres.

De todos os lados do espectro político, as mulheres receberam a mensagem de que suas preocupações não deveriam ser prioridade, mas permanecer uma mera distração na grande luta masculinista pós-revolucionária pelo poder político.

Nos meses que se seguiram aos protestos de março, o regime continuou a apertar seu domínio sobre a oposição política. Em agosto de 1979, o último dos principais jornais nacionais que não era controlado pelo estabelecimento foi fechado à força. A sede do Fada'iyan e do Mojahedin Khalgh foi tomada e suas publicações declaradas ilegais. Gangues de fanáticos religiosos continuaram a assediar e atacar regularmente livrarias, escritórios e manifestações de esquerda (Azari, 1980).

Em junho de 1981, a repressão do Estado havia erradicado com sucesso todas as formas de dissidência política aberta no país; a oposição foi levada à clandestinidade ou ao exílio, milhares de opositores e ativistas foram presos e muitos outros assassinados. A longa guerra de oito anos com o Iraque ajudou a consolidar ainda mais o estado, fornecendo-lhe um poderoso grito de guerra.

Também proporcionou uma oportunidade para as milícias religiosas se transformarem em uma força militar de pleno direito chamada Exército dos Guardas Revolucionários (Sepah e Pasdaran e Enghelabi), elevando o número total das forças armadas do regime islâmico para mais de meio milhão.

A supressão do ativismo político pelo regime continuou ao longo dos anos de guerra. Entre 1981 e 1985, mais de 8.000 opositores foram executados pelos tribunais revolucionários. As vítimas incluíam membros do Mojahedin, Fada'iyan, Tudeh, Frente Nacional e ativistas curdos. Muitos, incluindo líderes do Tudeh, foram forçados a aparecer na televisão nacional para se retratar de suas antigas opiniões políticas.

O derramamento de sangue final ocorreu imediatamente após o fim da guerra em 1988, quando mais de 2.800 prisioneiros políticos foram executados sem jul-

gamento em um período de quatro semanas e seus corpos despejados em valas comuns. Na época da morte de Khomeini em junho de 1989, sua república islâmica havia sido expurgada de todos os sinais de oposição esquerdista e nacionalista secular (Abrahamian, 2018).

A década de repressão política, que ficou conhecida na história iraniana contemporânea como o reinado do terror, afetou severamente o movimento de mulheres. Como mencionado anteriormente, a maioria das mulheres ativistas era afiliada a grupos marxistas (e, em menor grau, nacionalistas seculares) e, portanto, sofria a mesma punição que seus colegas homens por serem 'criminosos'. Após o aniquilamento das forças nacionalistas marxistas e seculares, foi a vez da oposição islâmica.

O movimento islâmico das mulheres, que se tornou cada vez mais vocal sobre as questões das mulheres e fez lobby extensivo pela preservação dos direitos legais concedidos às mulheres nos anos imediatos após a revolução, foi intimidado ao silêncio. No final da década de 1980, uma facção moderada e muito menos expressiva do movimento islâmico de mulheres ressurgiu. Enquanto as primeiras feministas islâmicas, como Azam Taleghani e Zahra Rahna-vard, se recusaram terminantemente a se associar ao movimento secular das mulheres, elas criticaram a imposição forçada do hijab e

defenderam suas próprias ideias sobre a 'verdadeira' visão do Islã para as mulheres na sociedade. As interpretações posteriores do movimento de mulheres islâmicas, no entanto, mostraram-se ainda mais limitadas em escopo e alcance.

A hipersensibilidade do governo à questão de gênero, juntamente com a contínua repressão violenta de qualquer forma de oposição política nas últimas três décadas, minou o movimento das mulheres a ponto de quase aniquilá-lo. O ativismo das mulheres no Irã foi atomizado e individualizado em um grau sem precedentes. É, portanto, por definição, impossível identificar um movimento abrangente de mulheres nas décadas do pós-guerra.

Os objetivos perseguidos por mulheres ativistas dentro do Irã também variaram consideravelmente dependendo do clima político, desde fazer lobby para a melhoria das leis de família e dos direitos constitucionais das mulheres até fazer campanha pela libertação de prisioneiros políticos. A ascensão temporária ao poder de moderados como Khatami e Rouhani permitiu articulações limitadas das demandas das mulheres, mas sempre em face da oposição das forças conservadoras dominantes que estavam ansiosas para desfazer quaisquer conquistas feitas em nome das mulheres assim que eles retomassem o controle do estado.

Um exemplo recente disso é a aprovação de uma nova lei sob Raisi, o atual presidente da República Islâmica, em 2021, que proíbe os provedores de saúde pública de oferecer contracepção gratuita e proíbe a esterilização voluntária. Isso é considerado um grande revés para a autonomia e integridade corporal das mulheres iranianas e seus anos de ativismo na área de direitos reprodutivos, cujas consequências, principalmente para as mais vulneráveis, como meninas e vítimas de abuso sexual, só serão desvendadas nos próximos anos.

Apesar dessas limitações, as mulheres iranianas continuam a resistir a estruturas de gênero opressivas. Recentemente, o movimento das mulheres iranianas se ramificou em novas e estimulantes direções políticas no exílio. O surgimento de novos modos de comunicação e a crescente popularidade das mídias sociais ajudaram a mobilizar uma nova geração de feministas iranianas dentro e fora do país.

A mídia social forneceu uma plataforma importante para a articulação coletiva das preocupações das mulheres e o lançamento de campanhas educativas e de conscientização sobre questões de gênero. Pela primeira vez, o feminismo iraniano adotou uma lente interseccional, construindo alianças com ativistas queer e trans e defendendo questões relativas a minorias raciais, étnicas e religiosas.

O surgimento do movimento iraniano #MeToo também forneceu uma oportunidade sem precedentes para mulheres iranianas de várias origens compartilharem publicamente relatos de abuso sexual, revelando a extensão esmagadora da violência de gênero que mulheres em todos os estratos sociais são submetidas. Em alguns casos, a exposição de agressores sexuais até resultou em suas prisões e indiciamentos no Irã (Ahmadi, 2023).

O nascimento do movimento Mulher, Vida, Liberdade, após o assassinato brutal de Jina (Mahsa) Amini enquanto estava sob custódia da polícia moral iraniana em setembro de 2022, abriu ainda mais um novo capítulo importante no ativismo feminista iraniano. Apelidado de revolução feminista do Irã, o movimento em curso adota o slogan feminista curdo de Jin, Jiyan, Azadi para priorizar as demandas de gênero, particularmente o direito à autonomia corporal para mulheres iranianas e pessoas não-conformantes de gênero, utilizando modos inovadores de resistência cotidiana (ibid.).

Essas novas ondas de ativismo feminista e construção de solidariedade, embora em seus estágios iniciais de desenvolvimento, estão criando terrenos promissores para avançar as causas políticas das mulheres e desafiar as forças masculinistas que até agora dominaram tanto o status quo político quanto sua oposição.

CONSIDERAÇÕES FINAIS

Narrar as atividades políticas das mulheres iranianas ao longo do século passado mostra que a participação das mulheres nos assuntos políticos do Irã não começou com sua presença em massa nas manifestações de rua que resultaram na derrubada do xá em 1979. Em vez disso, foram décadas de organização, mobilização e negociação em nome de mulheres ativistas que ativaram massas de mulheres e abriram caminho para seu envolvimento visível em eventos revolucionários.

Relatos históricos, muitas vezes, ignoram esse legado importante do movimento de mulheres iranianas do século XX, creditando a liderança carismática de Khomeini como o único fator que contribuiu para a mobilização em massa de mulheres, particularmente aquelas de origem trabalhadora e conservadora. Tais contos reducionistas lembram o essencialismo orientalista, que retrata as mulheres muçulmanas como recipientes passivos da política, que seguem cegamente a autoridade de homens religiosos em sua busca pelo poder político.

Este livro mostra que as mulheres iranianas foram tudo menos vítimas passivas e que suas contribuições e organizações políticas foram fundamentais para qualquer progresso feito em nome de movimentos sociopolíticos no Irã contemporâneo.

Desde a década de 1980, passos importantes foram dados por mulheres historiadoras para combater a natureza retalhada da história política das mulheres iranianas. Apesar desses esforços, as narrativas históricas dominantes continuam a enquadrar o papel das mulheres nos desenvolvimentos políticos do Irã do século XX como mera "participação", na melhor das hipóteses.

Os discursos nacionalistas e islâmicos em evolução em torno dos quais os principais desenvolvimentos políticos do século foram organizados, em geral, consideravam as mulheres como objetos de proteção, e não como sujeitos políticos. O trabalho de Afsaneh Najmabadi sobre a história das filhas de Quchan iluminou esses pontos cegos históricos ao traçar as origens de gênero do nacionalismo iraniano (1996; 1998). Najmabadi postula que, ao longo do movimento constitucional, a noção de 'país' (vatan) emergiu como uma entidade feminizada cuja autonomia dependia da proteção de homens patriarcais e patrióticos. A 'nação' (mellat) foi, por sua vez, mascu-

linizada como o sujeito agêntico encarregado de proteger tanto a soberania do país quanto a pureza de suas mulheres.

Os discursos nacionalistas da era constitucional, portanto, instrumentalizaram o corpo feminino (e seu correspondente Vatan), de modo a criar uma ampla simpatia pelas causas do nacionalismo e do constitucionalismo. Essa instrumentalização não resultou na melhoria das condições de opressão das mulheres ou na centralização de sua causa no movimento constitucionalista mais amplo. Na verdade, as histórias e as contribuições políticas das mulheres foram efetivamente apagadas da historicização e da memória coletiva da era constitucional, uma vez que serviram ao seu propósito de acordo com a mobilização de sentimentos nacionalistas de massa.

Ao longo do século XX, os corpos das mulheres continuaram a emergir como campos de batalha ideológicos e políticos contestados. Isso é especialmente evidente com relação à questão do hijab. A imposição vigorosa de Reza Shah do decreto de tirada do véu polarizou a sociedade iraniana e os ativistas dos direitos das mulheres. Também acrescentou combustível à oposição do clero conservador à modernização da posição social das mulheres, que enquadrava a emancipação das mulheres como um grito de secularização e desislamização.

Reza Shah, por sua vez, reprimiu o movimento independente de mulheres e despolitizou suas demandas. Mais tarde, ele criou uma associação de mulheres centralizada, sancionada pelo governo que controlaria e canalizaria as atividades políticas das mulheres de acordo com seu plano autoritário de modernização, enquanto continuava a repressão coercitiva de organizações de mulheres afiliadas politicamente e ativistas individuais.

Mohammad Reza Shah seguiu os passos de seu pai, centralizando ainda mais as organizações de mulheres e reprimindo a atividade política independente. Ao contrário de Reza Shah, que respondeu à dissidência política recorrendo principalmente à coerção violenta, Mohammad Reza Shah usou o método político da cenoura e da vareta (recompensa e punição) em sua cooptação do movimento das mulheres.

As mulheres ativistas que se aliaram aos planos de modernização do monarca foram absorvidas pelo aparato do estado, por meio do qual continuaram a fazer lobby para melhorias legais nas condições das mulheres. Duas conquistas notáveis em nome do movimento centralizado de mulheres durante a era Pahlavi II podem ser consideradas como a emancipação feminina e a Lei de Proteção à Família de 1975.

Como o último Xá do Estado Imperial, Mohammad Reza adotou uma estratégia de dividir para conquistar

em resposta ao movimento das mulheres. Como resultado, as mulheres ativistas foram colocadas umas contra as outras e ainda mais divididas em linhas ideológicas e de classe. Isso erradicou toda e qualquer possibilidade de construção de coalizão entre as mulheres e a centralização das preocupações das mulheres nos movimentos políticos mais amplos da era Pahlavi II.

O mesmo padrão de fragmentação e polarização pode ser observado entre as mulheres integrantes de grupos políticos de oposição no período pré-revolucionário. Embora as diferenças ideológicas entre as mulheres monarquistas e as mulheres ativistas no lado da oposição, particularmente na esquerda, fossem muitas vezes irreconciliáveis, as mulheres de esquerda compartilhavam um terreno ideológico comum o suficiente para formar uma frente unida na organização em torno da causa feminina. Isso, infelizmente, não foi alcançado devido à existência de pequenas rivalidades entre os grupos de oposição marxistas dos quais essas mulheres ativistas dependiam.

No nível interno, as organizações marxistas de oposição se recusaram a priorizar as questões das mulheres sobre as causas revolucionárias mais imediatas do anti-imperialismo e da luta contra a desigualdade de classe, e suas respostas às preocupações das mulheres permaneceram fragmentadas e simbólicas. Essa abordagem, cega

ao gênero da oposição marxista, continuou durante os primeiros anos da era pós-revolução e foi finalmente contestada quando o regime islâmico aplicou totalmente suas leis discriminatórias contra as mulheres.

Da mesma forma, durante a revolução de 1979, os corpos das mulheres, mais uma vez, ressurgiram como bases politizadas nas quais as forças revolucionárias islâmicas "reverteriam" os esforços de modernização do xá. O programa de islamização do regime pós-revolucionário visava especificamente os corpos das mulheres e as relações sociais. A oposição ao sexismo do novo regime disfarçado de islamização foi, por sua vez, enquadrada como 'antirrevolucionária' e pró-ocidente. Figuras religiosas que anteriormente elogiavam a participação heroica das mulheres nos eventos revolucionários e se gabavam do alto status das mulheres em uma sociedade islâmica, emergiram como oponentes ferrenhos da emancipação das mulheres quando no poder.

Assim como durante o reinado de Reza Shah, a questão do uso do véu tornou-se um ponto focal nos esforços do novo regime para consolidar seu poder. Ambos os regimes visaram os direitos das mulheres à autonomia corporal e recorreram a medidas enérgicas e repressivas para reduzir a resistência e garantir o cumprimento em massa.

Assim, um tema recorrente que pode ser observado em vários estágios da história iraniana contemporânea é o aparelhamento coercivo das causas e preocupações das mulheres por partes políticas interessadas, independentemente de suas posições religiosas e políticas, em direção a seus próprios ganhos políticos e a marginalização subsequente, e o apagamento das causas das mulheres, uma vez que elas não serviam mais às agendas políticas masculinistas mais amplas. Fica evidente que o gênero sempre foi simultaneamente politizado e apagado do debate político, um padrão que se mantém até hoje.

Reescrever as histórias contemporâneas de mobilização de baixo para cima, recentralizando as histórias e narrativas daquelas cujas vozes e lutas foram tornadas irrelevantes, continua sendo uma tarefa política pesada, mas vital. Aproveitando o poder e a sabedoria da experiência compartilhada, as feministas iranianas são capazes de reavaliar os modos políticos de nossas antepassadas e rearticular nossas demandas políticas de acordo com uma práxis libertadora radical. Além disso, há lições importantes a serem extraídas das lutas de justiça social de mulheres em todo o mundo.

Os ensinamentos inestimáveis das feministas negras sobre a interseccionalidade e as formas interconectadas pelas quais vários eixos de poder e privilégio moldam as

identidades e experiências vividas das mulheres continuam sendo fontes de inspiração notáveis.

A história nos mostra repetidamente que os movimentos de justiça social que falham em problematizar suas hierarquias internas de poder podem se tornar locais onde as estruturas de poder coercitivas são reproduzidas. A adoção de abordagens estreitas de eixo único para a organização política, como foi o caso dos grupos de oposição marxistas no Irã pré e pós-revolucionário, resulta ainda na periferização das vozes das mulheres, minorias étnicas e pessoas cuir, e mina a sustentabilidade do movimento e a radicalidade de suas reivindicações. Somente através da busca de uma práxis feminista verdadeiramente interseccional e construção de solidariedade entre várias classes, gêneros, sexualidades e etnias, o movimento de mulheres iranianas pode liberar seu verdadeiro potencial transformador.

REFERÊNCIAS

Abrahamian, E. (2021). *Iran between two revolutions*. Princeton University Press.

Abrahamian, E. (2018). *A history of modern Iran*. Cambridge University Press.

Abrahamian, E. (1989). *The Iranian Mojahedin*. Yale University Press.

Abrahamian, E. (1985). The guerrilla movement in Iran, 1963–77. *Iran* (pp. 149–174). Palgrave Macmillan, London.

Abrahamian, E. (1979). The causes of the constitutional revolution in Iran. *International Journal of Middle East Studies*, 10(3), 381–414.

Abrahamian, E. (1978). Iran: the Political Challenge. *Middle East Report*, no. 69, Julho-Agosto.

Abrahamian, E. (1970). Communism and communalism in Iran: The Tudah and the Firqah-i Dimukrat. *International Journal of Middle East Studies*, 1(4), 291–316.

Afary, J. (1996). *The Iranian Constitutional Revolution, 1906–1911*. New York.

Afary, J. (1989). On the origins of Feminism in early 20th-century Iran. *Journal of Women's History*, 1(2), 65–87.

Afshar, H. (1985). *Women, Work, and Ideology in the Third World*. London: Tavistock.

Afshar, H. (1981). The Position of Women in an Iranian Village. *Feminist Review*, no. 9.

Ahmadi, D. (2023). Standing on top of society's sexist load: Gatekeeping activism and feminist respectability politics in the case

of the Iranian MeToo Movement. *Women's Studies International Forum, 99*, 102765.

Azari, F. (1983). *Women of Iran: The Conflict with Fundamentalist Islam.* London: Ittaca Press.

Bamdad, B. A. M. (1977). *From Darkness Into Light: Women's Emancipation in Iran.* Editado e traduzido por F. R. C. Bagley. New York: Exposition Press.

Bayat-Philipp, M. (2013). 15 Women and Revolution in Iran, 1905–1911. *Women in the Muslim world* (pp. 295–308). Harvard University Press.

Kashani-Sabet, F. (2005). Patriotic womanhood: The culture of feminism in modern Iran, 1900–1941. *British Journal of Middle Eastern Studies, 32*(1), 29–46.

Mahdi, A. A. (2004). The Iranian women's movement: A century long struggle. *The Muslim World, 94*(4), 427–448.

Millett, K. (1982). *Going to Iran.* Coward, McCann & Geoghegan.

Najmabadi, A. (1998). *The story of the daughters of Quchan: Gender and national memory in Iranian history.* Syracuse University Press.

Najmabadi, A. (1996). "Is our name remembered?": Writing the history of Iranian constitutionalism as if women and gender mattered. *Iranian Studies, 29*(1-2), 85–109.

Najmabadi, A. (1993). Zanha-yi Millat: women or wives of the nation? *Iranian Studies, 26*(1-2), 51–71.

Najmabadi, A. (1987). *Land reform and social change in Iran* (pp. 50–168). Salt Lake City: University of Utah Press.

Paidar, P. (1995). *Women and the Political Process in Twentieth-Century Iran*. Cambridge Middle East studies, Vol. 1.

Sanasarian, E. (1982). *The Women's Rights Movement in Iran Mutiny, Appeasement, and Repression from 1900 to Khomeini*. New York: Praeger.

Siavoshi, S. (1990). *Liberal Nationalism in Iran: The Failure of a Movement*. Boulder: Westview Press.

Tabari, A. (1980). The enigma of veiled Iranian women. *Feminist Review*, 5(1), 19-31.